The Revolution of 2010

The Fight for Freedom, Values, and the American Way

CARLOS CARDOSO

iUniverse, Inc.
New York   Bloomington

iUniverse books may be ordered through booksellers or by contacting:

iUniverse
1663 Liberty Drive
Bloomington, IN 47403
www.iuniverse.com
1-800-Authors (1-800-288-4677)

ISBN: 978-1-4502-5466-3 (pbk)
ISBN: 978-1-4502-5467-0 (ebk)

Library of Congress Control Number: 2010912268

Printed in the United States of America

iUniverse rev. date: 8/23/2010

To my father and my mother, who gave up all they had and all they knew so we could live free. Thanks also to God for guiding me and giving me the strength to see me through this journey. To my family, I thank them for their patience with me, as I worked to bring this adventure to fruition. To all my family and friends, who were there as my sanity check as I embarked on a brand-new adventure. Finally, to my brother Stu, who has always had faith in all that I have done. Without his support, this may not have been possible.

Preface

There are several reasons I decided to write this book. First, I could not sit idly by while our government began to change drastically before my very eyes. Our government became arrogant and passed laws with long-term consequences for our nation against the people's overwhelming wishes. I felt the beginning of the loss of individual freedoms and liberties we have all taken for granted except for those brave men and women who risk their lives to protect and defend our Constitution. I feel a need to say something to unite our people in a direction of limited government and maximum liberties for every American citizen. We face too many dangers to remain divided any longer.

I feel compelled to write this book because of my own family history, which gives me a unique perspective on America, what it is and what it stands for. My father was studying to be a surgeon in Cuba when Fidel Castro took power. He and my mom decided to leave Cuba so their son would not be raised by the state. They were forced to leave everything of value behind, including my mom's engagement and wedding rings. I am the oldest of five boys, and I emigrated here when I was ten months old. My dad worked hard to learn; he spoke and wrote in English as well as anyone. He worked for a pharmaceutical company and supported five boys and a stay-at-home mom. I have a wife and three children of my own and feel I could do no less than to make my voice heard, proposing a difficult yet, I believe, commonsense approach to winning back our country from our government and remembering our roots and who we are as a nation before it was too late. The constitution is in danger, under attack by an ever expanding and unresponsive government. Passing far reaching legislation clearly against the wishes of a significant majority of Americans that infringes on our individual liberty. No branch of

Government has the power to change the constitution; this can only be accomplished through the amendment process. I studied our founding and our Founding Fathers. Their words are out there for us all to see and heed. America needs to learn who we are and how we came to where we are. Go to the library, check the Internet, learn why America has been special and able to accomplish so much for such a relatively young nation.

I could not see my country bankrupted for my children and their children for our own selfish reasons. Liberty, the foundation of human rights, came from God, and yet we seem to forget that. Our nation is humanity's hope for a bright future for the people of our planet. We have always been leaders to the world, in times both good and bad, and have always persevered to victory against dangers to freedom. I had to do this for my children, even though they don't yet understand. America, I urge you to learn from your own history and fight to preserve what our Founding Fathers envisioned: a country strong, proud, and free. The last bastion of hope for a dangerous world, a place where all who long for freedom can look up to. I feel we are at a crossroads in history, that our choices must be made extremely carefully, for there is a path back to who we are. And that's where we must go. Look at your children and ask yourself what will you tell them once history has unfolded, where were you when it all happened? What did you do: were you active, did you see it unfolding? Where you oblivious, caught up in your own little world? Did you stand up for our God-given rights, or did you watch them slip away? Hopefully, this book will move you to stand up when it counts now, assuring that we face our children knowing we had made the right choices when it mattered most. We must assure them the blessings of liberty, which is their birthright and our American civic duty to protect.

Contents

CHAPTER 1

2010 Defending Our Founding Ideals

The American Revolution did not begin with the first shot fired from a gun. Nor did it end with the defeat of the most powerful military power on the face of the Earth at that time, accomplished by an ill-equipped, poorly trained, and hopelessly overmatched group of citizens who relied on faith and principles. The Revolution began much earlier, as an idea that the government was unresponsive to the people's needs, unrepresentative of the people's views, and gave them no voice or ability to seek redress from unfair practices, which denied them their basic liberties.

The Revolution began with the idea that government gained its power through the consent of the governed. This idea was well articulated by Thomas Paine in his publication *Common Sense*. He quoted scriptures and history regarding the illegitimacy of kings having rights over their fellow men. He especially questioned the right of succession. He also laid out a system of representative government accountable to the people it served as a whole, not believing a small group should be entrusted to control decisions for the common good.

This left our Founding Fathers to gather together and pledge their allegiance, fortunes, and fates to one another, to seek divine guidance and seek independence from England. This decision was not one taken lightly, as many were men of education and means. Their decision placed them in grave danger, but they held to the truths they held dear: man receives inalienable rights directly from the Creator, and no man has the right to take these away, no matter what his station or title in life.

The Revolution began formally with the Founding Fathers seeking divine inspiration as well as His blessing in crafting the Declaration of Independence and culminated in the Constitutional Congress, which produced the Constitution of the United States. The constitution established the government as a republic rather than a democracy. Though both are similar, a republic is founded on the principle of individual sovereignty. A democracy allows 51 percent of the people to take away the rights of 49 percent of the people. Our republic was founded on the principle that we receive our right to liberty from God. The government is responsible to protect these rights. It is a testament to the wisdom and foresight of our Founding Fathers that our nation would be established as a republic ensuring that we would never live under the dictates of a ruler.

The members of our military as well as our elected officials in the House, the Senate, our president and vice president swear an oath to the best of their ability to preserve, protect, and defend the Constitution.

As you read this book, I hope you will take the time to read our founding documents as well as Thomas Paine's *Common Sense.* It is important for all Americans to understand who we are and where we came from as a people and a nation. I also urge you to get involved in the political process and contact your elected officials to ensure that your voice is heard. And if your representatives do not do our bidding as our public servants, we must let them know that we will exercise our right at the ballot box to vote them out and vote people into office regardless of party affiliation who will help us take back our government. The 2010 elections is a battle to validate our American Revolution, it is our duty to unite and win the battle, as we seek to hold our government accountable to the oaths of office they all took by voting for candidates who pledge to uphold our constitution and principles we, the people, demand.

My purpose in writing this book is to begin public discourse on a course of action to win back our country from the special interests and corruption that plagues present-day Washington, D.C. I will be brief and concise, so every American can find time in the course of our increasingly busy lives to read these words and consider their merit.

I lay out a commonsense approach to what our candidates must pledge to capture the political grassroots movements of discontent sweeping our great nation. This movement, outside of our mainstream political parties, must not be ignored. The candidates in 2010 must put country before local issues and party affiliation. They must be people serving not for personal gain or to become rich but to be the public servants they are supposed to be.

They must understand the role of government and its limitations in usurping the individual liberties of the citizenry they serve. Politicians must provide us with transparency and accountability and restore our faith in our government through guaranteeing that our constitutional rights are not abrogated or weakened in any way. They must affirm the vision of our Founding Fathers and the free market system that rewards hard work, entrepreneurial risks, and creativity, and all according to their merits.

This is the greatest nation the Earth has ever known, but it is in danger of straying from its foundations. It runs the risk of self-destruction through forgetting what brought us to prominence. It risks losing the blessings of liberty for ourselves and our posterity, which many have fought and died to protect over the centuries.

I hope you will find the concepts in this book helpful, as we are engaged to win the battle of 2010, the ongoing fight for freedom, traditional American values, and the validation of our great American Revolution and our American way of life. We have been the envy of the world, as people from all over the world come here, seeking freedom from oppression, the blessings of liberty that so many of us take for granted, and their chance at the American dream for themselves and their families.

The elections of 2010 represent a watershed moment in history that could decide not only the fate of this great country, but also the future of Western Civilization, the direction of the free world, and our position of preeminence in the world. As Thomas Paine wrote so prophetically in *Common Sense*, "The cause of America is, in a great measure, the cause of all mankind. Our fate is in our own hands, no power on Earth can conquer America if she does not conquer herself through timidity or by delaying action."

Now, as we see the direction our country is headed, it is time for us to stand up, make our voices heard, and take our country back to the roots that made this country great. We must accept the call to action, to take the initiative to protect ourselves aggressively against all our enemies, and to name them boldly for who they are. First and foremost, Islamic terrorists who seek to destroy us and the world, if necessary, to impose their will against all who would oppose their system of beliefs and justice.

The government must first fulfill their primary purpose of providing for the common defense. We must acknowledge, though, that those in power have failed us by trying to minimize what we face. The administration avoids using the phrase "war on terror" to avoid upsetting those very countries' leaders, who have promoted and supported the export of this extremist view of Islam. This time of political correctness at the cost of our security must end now.

We must also act swiftly to right the bankrupting of America and save our nation and the future of our children, grandchildren, and great grandchildren. This is our call to action and why we cannot delay beyond 2010. This is our chance, before it is too late and the damage to our government becomes irreparable. We cannot continue to allow one group to control Congress and the executive branch with filibuster and veto-proof majorities that conduct our business behind closed doors and are unresponsive to our concerns and oblivious to our voices. The only government business that reasonably should be conducted in secrecy from the American people are matters of national security that would compromise our ability to defend ourselves from our potential and real enemies. All domestic issues must be honestly and openly debated and then our elected officials held accountable for their actions. The times we live in, with instant communication capabilities, demands transparency and the ability of our will being done. The availability of polls, emails from concerned citizens and constituents gives our elected officials the ability to keep a constant feel of the opinions of the people, voting accordingly is their responsibility.

We must also be vigilant of those who believe that big government is the answer to our problems that government should decide for us, as a group what is in our best interests, thus diminishing our individual rights. This is exactly what our Founding Fathers so courageously opposed. They took their stand against seemingly impossible odds that our cause would be victorious, because our cause was just. They believed that the Creator would look with favor on our endeavors and ultimately bless us with our freedom and individual liberties. They had faith that our Revolution would lead to a form of government better than anything seen before in history. Thomas Jefferson said, "Yet with all its defects and with those of our particular governments, the inconveniences resulting from them are so light in comparison with those existing in every other government on earth that our citizens may certainly be considered as in the happiest political situation which exists."[1] We can never take our liberties or our blessings for granted. We must cherish them and do all we can to protect them against all enemies, foreign or domestic.

It has come to us now, in this time in history, to restore our country to its roots. We must be the beacon of freedom and individual liberties guaranteed by our Constitution and given to us by our Creator. We must stand together to regain our principles. We must acknowledge that we are responsible to use our God-given liberties to pursue happiness, and we alone can find our destiny based on our actions and decisions. That government's role in our life should be limited in scope and power. We face many grave challenges in this time, as we have throughout our history. We need to understand the urgency of our situation and united fight to regain our place in the community of nations. America has always been a country under God, and as such, if we can regain our understanding of this unique relationship, we can remain mankind's shining example of truth, liberty, and equal justice for all. We must preserve the America that exemplifies the best hope for all who seek to join us in the cause of freedom and liberty, giving hope to those around the world who seek to live in our land of opportunity and join us to secure peace and prosperity for us and our posterity.

May history find us worthy and say that this generation of Americans faced our challenges with faith, courage, and determination and once again prevailed against those who would threaten us, our way of life, and our republican system of government. That we stood as one and conquered the challenges we faced, once again leading the world to prosperity. We can only accomplish this by facing our problems now and as our Founding Fathers did, and leaving this country a stronger and better place for our children. This must be our mission: to persevere with fortitude and character, making the tough choices that will lead to a brighter future for our children. This is our moment; this is our turn to seek a commonsense approach to taking back our government from the special interests that are working to take from us what God has given us, to once again raise our voices until they can no longer be ignored, and for our elected officials to follow our Constitution and honor the values and principles on which this great nation was founded. We must act now before it is too late, and our children grow up in a world devoid of individual liberty. We must turn our government back to a responsible path that will lead us to the bright future we owe our children and grandchildren. We cannot sit idly by, as the stakes have never been higher. Should we fail, we will be judged harshly by history, and rightly so.

Notes

1. Thomas Jefferson to Edward Carrington. (Aug. 4, 1787. ME 6:227) http://etext.virginia.edu/jefferson/biog/lj20.htm, accessed December 18, 2009.

CHAPTER 2

God's Place in Our Country

The history of the new world and its colonization by England was in essence an exodus of people fleeing England to escape religious persecution. The colonies, as they began to be populated and overcame the initial challenges of simple survival, began to thrive and set up a system of representative government modeled loosely after the English bicameral model. Eventually, the number of colonies grew until there were thirteen at the time of the American Revolution. Throughout this period, the people were very cognizant of the need to build a society based on religious tolerance. Thomas Paine wrote, "It is the will of the Almighty, that there should be diversity of religious opinions among us: It affords a larger field for our Christian kindness. Were we all of one way of thinking, our religious dispositions would want matter for probation; and on this liberal principle, I look on the various denominations among us, to be like children of the same family, differing only, in what is called their Christian names."

This common experience eventually led to the concept of separation of church and state. This was not intended to remove God from our government or society but instead to ensure that no official religion be established. That religion needs to stay out of politics, as Thomas Paine wrote specifically to the Quakers, "Sincerely wishing, that as men and Christians, ye may always fully and uninterruptedly enjoy every civil and religious right; and be, in your turn, the means of securing it to others; but that the example which ye have unwisely set, of mingling religion with politics, may be disavowed and reprobated by every inhabitant of America."

This separation was meant to guarantee the rights of all Americans to worship as they saw fit, without fear of persecution, while admonishing religious leaders to stay out of strictly political debates. He differentiated between civil and religious rights as they are separate with their own individual responsibilities. Though we have an aversion to violence as a people because we understand the Creator surely wishes no harm to any of his children, He understands that right must be fought for and that evil must be confronted and defeated.

Over the years, we have allowed the courts to remove God and religion from all public entities. This was not the intention of our Founding Fathers. They were keenly aware of the need to seek and keep God's favor upon our cause in the pursuit of freedom and liberty. They understood that our country would only be blessed with liberty, freedom, and prosperity by seeking God's favor upon our nation. They felt their cause just and that God would intervene on our behalf. To this end, our country has always fought as a force for good in the world and not as a conqueror. This country was founded on Christian principles, and it was intended that it always follow this path, though without naming God by the labels of any organized religion or by intolerance toward any religion or lack thereof.

This ideal of seeking God's blessings can be seen in all the references to God and the Creator in our founding documents, our national buildings in our nation's capital, as well as the simple motto on all of our monetary denominations, the simple yet eloquent saying, In God We Trust. This can be seen most clearly when one looks above the Supreme Court Building in Washington, D.C. The center of the depiction is of Moses with the Ten Commandments, bringing them down from God. We are a country based on laws, righteousness, integrity, honesty, and above all else, an unshakeable faith that has made us invincible.

We as Americans are, by a large majority, a people who believe in God. If we are to regain our moral standing and God's continued blessings on our nation, we must strive to fight the wave of political correctness that has overrun our great country. We the majority can no longer remain silent to appease a small but vocal minority who have fought hard to remove God from our lives. Americans believe in God by an overwhelming majority, yet we must remain silent because a few would disagree? I would think most Americans would agree that the Founding Fathers would say that civil discourse on any subject, especially religion, is our right. This is directly what led to our country's founding and the shape our government would take. Our forefathers' common bond was being religious but not of a mandatory national religion; it was one of individual conscience and the right to choose. We were a grateful nation for all the blessings God had bestowed on us.

This is why we must insist that our leaders understand and pledge to fight to continue to seek God's blessings for ourselves and our posterity. We must insist that they fight to keep the spirit of God, however we may perceive Him, alive and well respected by our nation. We should continue to seek His wisdom and guidance as we make our way through an extremely dangerous world filled with people intent on carrying out unimaginable evil deeds to advance their agendas for world domination.

We are faced with evil forces that hate our freedom and religious tolerance, do not value human life as we do, and are willing to use any means at their disposal to destroy us and build a world that is the antithesis of that for which we stand. Now more than ever, we need people who are unafraid to rebuke publicly those who would try to change our traditional values of God and country. We need leaders who will seek God's guidance and wisdom as we go through the many challenges that we face as a nation.

I do not mean our politicians are expected to follow any religious agenda or be part of any particular faith. They must, however, understand our history and our traditions, and help the majority keep God alive against the forces that seek to drive Him out of our country entirely. I would expect them to pledge to keep In God We Trust on all our official currency, to keep the words "One nation under God" in our Pledge of Allegiance. This pledge is important in keeping true to our country's core values and traditional way of life: our true freedoms come from the Creator, not the government.

God gave us these rights. The government's responsibility was to protect them, not pretend that they decided to give us rights not mentioned in our Bill of Rights and protected by the Constitution.

The beauty and wisdom of the Constitution is that it allowed for amendments to face changes in the future that could not be foreseen or were politically impossible to pass at that time. Any additional rights given to us by God, we as a people saw as moral and necessary, could be added through the process of amending the Constitution. This process was deliberately designed to require ratification by a two-thirds majority of not only the House and Senate but also by ratification by three-fourths of the state legislatures.

CHAPTER 3

Freedom of Speech and the Bill of Rights

Freedom of speech by individuals and the media, including on the Internet, is constitutionally protected by the Bill of Rights and must continue to be. It cannot be legislated or regulated away. The Bill of Rights in its entirety must be preserved, protected, and defended against all enemies, foreign and domestic. All branches of the government, including the judiciary, must take their solemn oath and do all in their power to protect the freedoms guaranteed us by the Bill of Rights. It is their sworn duty to God and the people to protect the gifts of life and individual human rights that Americans have as the cornerstone of our society.

Government must respect the right of the people to assemble peacefully to ensure our voices cannot be ignored. Quoting Thomas Paine's writings in *Common Sense*, "It is not in numbers but in unity, that our great strength lies; yet our present numbers are sufficient to repel the force of all the world."

The media must truthfully report what transpires for our leaders, our people, and the world to see. Our voices should be raised in all manners available to us, including calling, e-mailing, petitioning, or visiting our elected officials in open forums or at their offices to make our positions clear on the issues. We must openly debate the questions of the day. Our elected leaders owe us the right to be heard and heeded, less they face the possibility of removal from office by all legal means available to us.

The Tea Party movement has been a manifestation of the extreme dissatisfaction within our nation of the current policies being implemented by the current administration and the Democratic majority in both houses of the U.S. Congress. Yet, this movement is not a concoction of the opposition party, whose leadership has been unable to effectively articulate a strategy or propose or implement a course of action to capture the reigns of this growing movement.

Instead, a void has been created where ordinary citizens must step up to provide a vision and a clarity of purpose, and seek to actively promote change in a way that could ultimately lead to the demise of the two-party system to which we're accustomed. Ordinary citizens may find themselves organizing and volunteering to work for candidates who may or may not be associated with the leadership of either major party. They may even find themselves running for offices they may never had aspired to, just because the level of trust and approval of the current Congress is such that incumbents may not have the advantages they may had enjoyed in the past, especially against political newcomers in races at the local, state, and federal levels.

New candidates must pledge to honor their oath of office and work to preserve our liberties, heed our wishes, and enact laws that are constitutional and for the common good. They must work to repeal laws that are contrary to the common good and never place anything above their duty to God and country. Remember, they swear their oath with a hand on the Bible.

This duty must also be recognized and understood by us, their constituents, who must understand that what may be good for a district, a town, city, or state must be weighed on whether it is in the national interest. If it is not, the national interest is of primary importance, and our national leaders will be held accountable according to these criteria.

Incumbents holding onto power because it gave an area an edge at the expense of others due to seniority is not in the national interest. Leadership positions on congressional committees are currently led by the ranking member of the majority party not by any other criteria. Seniority does not necessarily mean that person is qualified to lead.

It should not, therefore, enter into the merits of issues being debated or voted on by our elected officials. The power of the people must be validated by our elected officials' actions on our behalf. Their decisions must be explained fully to us prior to voting on measures so that we the people can see that they are truly promoting the general welfare of our republic according to their sworn duties. This includes debates on bills, including all proposed amendments. C-SPAN has the ability to carry these debates, as do several other media outlets, such as the Internet and cable or satellite TV. We should not, ever again, allow a group of our senators to gather behind closed doors to craft a deal. Never again, should senators gather behind closed doors, craft a bill, and then end debate without the citizens and the entire Senate being privy to a bill already passed by the House, also completely by one party. The nation was assured by the leadership of the Senate, Senator Harry Reid of Nevada, that he couldn't discuss the terms of the deal but that the American public would love it once we learned what was in it. Speaker of the House Nancy Pelosi of California said virtually the same thing. This commonly referred to as the health care reform bill became H.R. 4872, The Patient Protection and Affordable Care Act.

The promise of transparency was reneged on by our government. We were promised access to the legislation being considered prior to its being voted on, but in this case, it was hidden from our view, even though our president, during his campaign, promised several times it would be televised on C-SPAN. No debate ever occurred on a deal that was unseen by the complete Senate. This bill, when enacted and signed into law by a president who has made it the cornerstone of his campaign and political agenda, could conceivably take over a significant portion of America's economy and endanger our liberties. All this while the president has been pondering for months a request for more troops by his appointed general in the war in Afghanistan, in the face of the possibility that the war could be lost.

This is incredulous, when within the first year of this administration; there have been several terrorist attacks on and above American soil. The first, being the Fort Hood shooting where thirteen people were killed and thirty-two left wounded. The Pentagon report cited missed opportunities and emails to a Yemeni cleric inquiring on jihad. The second, was the plot to blow up a plane on Christmas Day with an underwear bomb. Again in this case the government had received warnings on this individual and allowed him to board a plane bound for Detroit. Ironically, the first two since soon after the shot heard round the world, signaling the beginning of World War III—September 11, 2001. I have felt that way since then. The naysayers and politically correct can call me a fear monger, a favorite tactic of those who seek to minimize our power by trying to dismiss our views by ridiculing our positions, but how many countries since 2001 are currently actively involved in antiterrorist operations around the globe? I believe we could be one incident away from global escalation of hostilities around the world.

The first two situations were initially downplayed by government officials. The most recent they had to label as a terrorist attack, much to their chagrin, when the suspect's claims had been legitimized by al Qaeda, which claimed responsibility. The first was belatedly labeled as such in the face of known associations prior to the attack, because of the policies of this administration. They rationalized their terminology by calling terrorism a tactic and terror a state of mind that Americans do not give in to fear. Though the statement is true on face value, it misses the point that terrorists and their organizations are our primary enemies.

Here, our civic duty as citizens who seek to protect freedom of speech must be to hold the media at large responsible for not reporting or investigating on stories for which there is available information. This should be done not to scare the American public, since we have proven throughout our history we are not a nation that can be motivated into acquiescence out of fear. We have shown ourselves a nation that responds with determination, strength, and unity, seeking justice rather than vengeance and invoking the moral right of self-defense.

We must embark on the path of activism and send those organizations that have failed us in their roles as watchdogs a loud and clear message. A flood of calls, letters, and e-mails threatening boycotts of their programming could put at risk the sponsorship they rely on to operate. We must act by making our voices heard. Through our acting together until we cannot be ignored, the media must be put on notice of our expectations of them in a democratic republic and reminded that their role is to disseminate information to us in a fair and timely manner. If our marches on our nation's Capital can be ignored, would they be at the offices of the networks that have failed us? The newspapers, magazines, and company advertisements that fail to meet our expectations must also be held accountable.

I, for one, find the "Go Forth" commercials for the Levi Jeans Company disturbing. The sign lit up, spelling out America, leaning on an angle in water signifies to me or seems to imply our fall from greatness. I would expect that many who have seen this particular commercial question the message intended to be sent and find it offensive. I again advocate that we be the silent majority no longer.

We will be respected and treated with such by all who would seek our support. So, we as citizens must fight for our American values by speaking out loudly against any agenda that tries to promote us as powerless when we are anything but. All power is given to the people by our Creator and, as such, is powerful beyond measure. We can affect political power over the government, media, and corporations. We can affect them politically and economically, and hold them accountable to us if they wish our consent and our financial backing.

Last, the government should fulfill its responsibility to investigate the causes of security lapses that place us at risk. Political correctness must be challenged and exposed as the failure that it is. We need to speak plainly and mean what we say. Our government must do the same. They must do all in their power to end this ridiculous form of censorship of speech that directly leads to failed policies and protocols that endanger our interests and us. To do less is a travesty and an insult to our intelligence. Department of Homeland Security Secretary Janet Napolitano should have been fired after her comments on the so-called "Christmas Bomber." For her to say the system had worked when it clearly failed was an affront to the American people. If her idea of a working system is a vigilant non-American thwarting a would-be terrorist on an airplane above a major American city, she is obviously clueless or believes the American public to be.

Legislation needs to be put out there for all of us to see. It cannot be explained as being too complex, that they didn't read the whole thing, that their staff reviewed it, or that we wouldn't understand. So, they'll do what's best for us. If it's better for us, tell us how. Tell us what it costs and why we need it now! State your case and then listen to us. Wasn't that the reason we were promised transparency, so we could decide and speak, so our voices would be heard and our wishes be honored? Thomas Jefferson said, "All tyranny needs to gain a foothold is for people of good conscience to remain silent."[1] You, the reader, contemplate and decide what, if any, action to take. If you agree, time will be short, as November 2010 quickly approaches.

We cannot afford to remain silent. The time is now for us to stand with one united voice and end the abuses of power and disregard for the Constitution, which is and always shall remain the supreme law of this land. The world's beacon of hope for human rights and liberties cannot flicker or be darkened with the world in the peril it is in now. Freedom and all of our basic human rights are not gifts to us from our government; they come from the Creator and, as such, must be defended now. The stakes for us and the implications for the world make our duty clear. We must unite and step up to make our voices heard. We must take our country back from those who would abuse their power, ignore justice, and fail in their basic duties to us, the American people; back from those who are not ensuring domestic tranquility, providing for the common defense, promoting the general welfare, or securing the blessings of liberty to ourselves and our posterity.

Notes

1. Thomas Jefferson. BrainyQuote.com, Xplore Inc, 2010. http://www.brainyquote.com/quotes/quotes/t/thomasjeff136431.html, accessed July25, 2010.

CHAPTER 4

Term Limits

Term limits need to be put in place to reduce the power of incumbency. We do not want lifetime politicians in place, with a long history of fund-raising and special-interest group and lobbyist ties, and, in turn, expectations. We need to have politicians who are beholden to the people, the citizens, and understand that their actions while in office will be under intense scrutiny. Politicians who serve for a short time out of a feeling of necessity or duty to country are the ones we need. People who do not seek a lucrative career by reaping the spoils that the system currently allows, building large war chests to ensure their reelection. We all know nothing in this life comes free; donors expect some favor for their cash and or fund-raising efforts.

The current system allows those who serve in Congress to be rewarded for their longevity by being appointed to higher levels on ever-more powerful committees that control increasingly larger portions of our budget. They can then funnel funding in whatever direction they see fit through their positions of influence and authority. For a long time, the American public has trusted our politicians in Washington or become apathetic to their work. The sheer volume of proposed bills and the language in which it was scripted leaves many Americans in a sense of complacency. The incredible exponential expansion of our national debt is a testament to our not paying attention to what has been done in our name by our elected officials at all levels of government.

The turnover of our representatives and senators is indeed the position our Founding Fathers advocated through their actions, and they would feel even more strongly about it in today's world, where so many more Americans are educated and capable. They considered public service a duty of a citizen to his country as a matter of honor. They considered it a privilege to serve with the motivation of advancing the causes of the common good.

Today's politicians need to comprehend that their duties while in a national position must be to put forward the interests of the nation as a whole, above a narrow view in which they serve the interests of their particular state or congressional district. This is not to say that the constituents who vote for them should be ignored or marginalized in any way. Their constituents' views should be included in any debate and voiced as such. Then the argument being debated should end with the representative's view on whether they agree with the consensus, explaining the reason why the person is convinced that his or her vote should be cast as yea or nay on any proposed legislation. They must also always remain accessible and helpful to their constituents and assist when they can. They must respond to their constituents' communications with answers to questions raised by them, regardless of whether they support their public policy stands.

Currently, the president is limited to two terms. George Washington, our beloved and first president, stepped down after two terms, saying it was enough and not wanting our country to trade one king for another. He understood that it was necessary for him to step down and set the example of the peaceful transfer of power through our constitutional right to choose our leaders through the use of secret ballots, tabulated and then validated by the Electoral College.

We now need term limits for all of our nationally elected leaders. I propose that Representatives be limited to five terms. This would allow for a maximum of ten years in office. Senators would be limited to two terms. This would allow them a maximum of twelve years in office. Our elected officials would be able to collect their pensions with a minimum of ten years of service, at the age of sixty-two, as set forth in the pension system currently in place for our government employees.

Again, we must decide if these elected officials are truly fulfilling their oaths of office and are worthy of serving the entire time to earn their pensions. They can still earn a pension with five years of service, at the age of sixty-five. If they do not, we must vote them out or remove them from office by any means legally available.

These positions are not to be taken lightly, and the media must use all means at their disposal to ensure that our elected officials are held accountable to the highest moral, ethical, and constitutionally legal standards. This is not a claim by the author to be perfect by any means. I, like all of us, have made my share of mistakes. I just hope that with the Good Lord's guidance, I may find the wisdom to give voice to our great country's principles in a manner that may move the electorate, you the citizens, to find your voice and save our nation from those who would harm us, all enemies, foreign and domestic. However, our elected officials, while in our employ, must rise above our human imperfections and be role models for us and our children.

The ability to be an elected official is and must be viewed as an honor by those who enter into positions to speak and legislate, govern and adjudicate. They must understand that their foremost obligation and responsibility is to uphold the Constitution. Term limits must be put in place, and potential candidates who seek our support must pledge to enact term limits no longer than discussed above. This means that only a truly excellent nationally elected official could serve no more than thirty eight years. That would be a maximum of ten years as a representative, twelve years as a senator, eight years as vice president and 8 years as president. The only exception would be Supreme Court Justices, who are appointed by the president, confirmed by the Senate, and serve for life, barring bad behavior, until they choose to retire.

Again, for those serving for such a long period, they must demonstrate the willingness and ability to serve the public good with distinction, honor, and conviction, and remain accountable to us at all times. They must conduct themselves with honesty, allowing us access to their deliberations, debates, and all matters being considered by the Congress. They must exhibit professional, ethical, and moral behavior throughout their tenure in office. They must prove that our trust in them is well deserved, or we will replace them with candidates whose word is their bond and their character is above reproach. Public officials must be people of integrity who you would trust to serve and always put American values, principles, and the defense of our Constitution above all else. These perilous times demand that we choose wisely in whom we place our trust to reduce the size and scope of the federal government while championing the cause of liberty.

We need to have all of our candidates for the positions of representatives and senators to pledge to put in place term limits. This is surely what our founding fathers intended and what we need today. This is something we will use to hold our elected officials accountable to us for the betterment of our great republic.

CHAPTER 5

Congressional Benefits

Members of Congress enjoy a good salary, way above what most of us can expect to earn. Representatives and senators currently earn an annual salary of $174,000. The minority and majority leaders each earn $193,400 per year, and the Speaker of the House earns $223,500 per year. They are also entitled to an annual cost of living increase and can vote themselves raises, but according to the Constitution, salaries cannot be increased in the current year. This is much higher than the national average salary of approximately $40,000, which we earn. They receive more than four times the national average for the honor and privilege of serving us. They need to put our and the nation's interests first, because we, in essence, hire them with our votes. They work for us.

On top of the compensation paid by us the taxpayers, members of Congress have the right to raise huge amounts of money for their reelection. They are free to use this money to strengthen their grip on power and influence, choose to save or spend money they receive from their fund-raising efforts at their discretion. Remember, again, the old saying that nothing comes free or without cost. Imagine multimillion-dollar accounts at their disposal, provided by special interests. There is another saying that comes to mind here: money talks. And where does that leave us? Do you really think our interests will be served over those who lavish huge sums of money on our elected officials?

Who do you know with the ability to tap into multimillion-dollar accounts? I don't know about you, but I don't personally know anyone. We have created a group of over privileged, overpaid people who are out of touch with what the common, hardworking, everyday Americans have to face in the challenges of raising a family and providing them with the advantage of a decent education, and hoping to pass on the American dream to our spouses, children, and grandchildren as it was passed down to us. The hope that they will be better off than we were: is that not what our parents sacrificed for us? Are we not paying too much for too little? I, for one, think that it is ludicrous, and we must act to hold our politicians accountable to act ethically, morally, honestly, and legally.

Public service should be done for honorable intentions and not for profit. Individuals who wish to profit from their abilities at this level should be successful leaders of companies that provide value to their owners, be they private or stockholders, and held accountable for the success of their efforts. They should also be people who provide job opportunities at a time when a job is one of the most precious commodities needed by the American people.

On health care, they have one huge perk that we wish we could have: they have the ability to use military hospitals free of charge. Imagine if we were to be stricken with an illness or injury and had the option available to use a hospital such as Walter Reed for any diagnostic testing, treatment, or procedure completely free of charge. This is not something that our veterans, who have risked life and limb for us, can automatically receive. Imagine a veteran who has been severely injured in fighting for our country having to pay for service, while our national elected leaders need not. Our service members who have sacrificed all to fight for our families' freedom are given less; this is an absolute travesty of justice and a disgrace. Yes, the basic health-care plan for members of Congress is a federal employee one with higher than average contributions, but their co-pays are lower than what average Americans pay.

On average, their retirement plans are estimated to be three to four times what we who pay for them receive.

The ways they receive compensation should be reevaluated. Transparency on their compensation including benefits, and fund-raising needs to be readily available to the citizens of this country, so we can decide what they should reasonably receive for their services. If the argument is we would lose valuable talent and experience due to decreased compensation, then so be it. Those who are in it for the money are not in it for us. Ben Franklin argued unsuccessfully that elected government officials receive no pay for their service. He understood that the motivation to public service should be out of duty to country.

Now, I certainly cannot subscribe to members not getting paid for their service, but their compensation should be reexamined. This, to me, also leads to the argument that campaign finance reform is urgently needed to keep our representatives working for us and with our national interests foremost in their minds as they vote. Transparency is desperately required so we know where the money comes from and how it is used. Election to public office should not be about who can raise the most money but, rather, who has the better vision, strategy, and plan to advance America's interests.

Members of Congress must demonstrate through their actions not their words true leadership we can follow and in which we can believe. They need to be willing to speak out against evil, wrongdoing, and corruption domestically and internationally, and vote in the interests of American citizens. They should be people who would advance and represent our historical values to the world and become the beacons for freedom, liberty, and human rights worldwide we've always been expected to be. We are, always have been, and must remain the hope of this world and cannot afford to lose our moral standing in believing that our God-given unalienable rights apply to every person on this planet. They must share the belief that all people are entitled to life, liberty, and the pursuit of happiness and the fruits of their labors.

So, consider that compensation for service should be fair and equitable, and any opportunity for us to try and take money out of the equation, and level the playing field where the ordinary citizen, if so moved, can compete with incumbents in elections to national, state and local offices needs to be examined. Ensuring that new blood can reinvigorate our democracy with fresh ideas and lawmakers are free to serve the people without unpaid debts to individuals or any special interests whose agendas differ from our needs and desires are vital to the health of our political system.

This has been a tough sell to both parties, as it threatens their ability to consolidate and hold onto power. Again, perhaps the paradigm has shifted, as Americans tired of business as usual speak out in indignation about where we've been led. All this counts as, what I believe, to be excessive compensation in direct opposition to keeping politicians reliant on our support if they are to remain in their positions until we vote them out or term limits kick in and they are forced to step down.

This may be the reason for the current of dissatisfaction with both parties. It could finally lead to the creation of a viable third party, supported by the common citizen tired of being ignored. The Tea Party movement has mobilized American people ready to affect real change, give new direction and the leadership of good people able to articulate their views and keep their word, of citizen public servants to be allowed to compete on convictions, ideals, and principles consistent with the beliefs of the majority of the citizens of this nation and not by who can control the airwaves with money.

Are there citizens out there ready to forgo the ubiquitous ability to accept money to further their own power and agendas, contrary to what we the people wish? We must believe that they are out there, that there always has been and always will be people who are willing to sacrifice their needs and ambitions for the national good. The Founding Fathers would be appalled at our current system, where money plays such a huge role not only in elections but also in policy decisions obviously not in the national interest.

Congressional benefits, whether they be high salaries, generous health-care and retirement benefits, or fund-raising activities, must be reviewed, revised, and controlled to ensure that the common good is the overriding motivation of our elected officials. They must be free of the undue influence of money from those who would attempt to ensure their interests come before ours. We live in a time of an unsustainable debt, and their total compensation package, including funds raised, must be examined and revised to more realistic levels, more in line with what we would consider fair for their services. We are entitled to this through our Constitution and should settle for no less. This will be a difficult task for many career politicians, who have gained wealth and power under the status quo. We must insist on their acceding to our wishes or stepping down. Politicians unwilling or unable to embrace this simple concept of cleaning our system of the corruption and influence peddling currently plaguing our political process must be removed from office, for they clearly do not understand their role or their duties. If our elected leaders can pass a law that affects us all—except them—and tells us it's in our best interest, they clearly cannot be trusted and should not be eligible for benefits of any kind.

Transparency is definitely required, so we can clearly see what our elected officials earn through all the income streams available to them. This includes a full accounting of their health-care benefits and how long they keep them. We also need to know what their pensions' amount to in annual payments and the longevity required to earn them. We are their bosses; we pay their salaries and benefits. Aren't we entitled to know what we are paying them? Would any of us hire an employee without knowing what they do to earn their money or even how much they earn? I certainly don't think so. It is time for us to see the money trail, so we can tailor it to a reasonable amount of compensation for their efforts and ensure the lawmakers are there for the right reason: to serve our country with honor and distinction. Only then can our political system be freed of the undue influence of special-interest groups instead of money from their constituents.

CHAPTER 6

The Census

The census is authorized by the Constitution in Article 1, Section 2: "The actual Enumeration shall be made within three Years after the first Meeting of the Congress of the United States, and within every subsequent Term of ten Years, in such Manner as they shall by Law direct. The Number of Representatives shall not exceed one for every thirty Thousand, but each State shall have at Least one Representative. Amendment 14, Section 2 further clarifies," The representatives shall be apportioned among the several states according to their respective numbers: "Counting the citizens 21 years of age." This is later amended in Article 26, Section 2, to change the voting age to eighteen.

The purpose of the census, then, should be to count citizens of the legal voting age in order to apportion congressional representation for each state, according to the number of citizens in all the states. This was done to ensure each state was given equal representation in the Congress based on its number of citizens. The key here is counting only citizens of the United States to apportion representation. Those who are below the voting age and those who are not citizens of this nation shall not count in this enumeration.

The purpose here is not to discount the entire population of diverse groups. Children below the voting age at the time of the census, for example, as well as legal immigrants should be counted, but separately. Many see this as an attempt to deny tax dollars used for any of these groups, but this argument is fundamentally flawed. Obviously, there is no truth to this argument, as there are several federal programs where taxpayer money is used to the betterment of our children and our communities as a whole. This does not, however, give them the right to representation in the government until citizenship is achieved either by attaining the age or choosing to join our citizenry through the process of naturalization, which confers on them the protection of our God-given rights as laid out in our Constitution until the next enumeration. They shall be counted in the next census and in subsequent ten-year increments.

The Census Bureau, however, plans to carry out its duties by sending packets in multiple languages to every home in America and not bothering to ask their citizenship status, little less verify it somehow. How, then, does it propose to fulfill the constitutional duty to count the citizenry of every state according to apportion proper congressional representation?

Clearly, they do not intend to do that. Their expressed mission is to determine the allocation of federal funds, according to the population and other factors they see fit to count in each part of the country, regardless of citizenship or immigration status. This argument is not to say that there is some merit in the information being gathered, though our privacy does seem to be infringed on by the scope of the questioning. However, what we, the citizens of this country, should first be asking ourselves is: How is our right to equal representation being impacted when the constitutionally stated purpose of the census is being ignored by those in power for their own political gain?

I again urge the citizens, the people of this great nation, to consider this, and as Thomas Jefferson wrote, "Question with Boldness" this undermining of our political rights. We must question our elected officials in Washington how we can allow our political landscape to be shaped in this manner, as they prepare to redraw the lines of our congressional districts without a proper census as laid out by our Constitution. What motivation do they have for ignoring our Constitution and the rights of the citizens of this country to be counted in a proper manner? We must remain silent no longer, less those currently in power consolidate their power by redrawing the map to try and ensure their continued grip on power for a decade or longer.

If you agree that this argument against the proposed census is valid, if you agree that these methods are illegal according to our Constitution, we must make our voices heard before it is too late. We must also fight the use of corrupt, questionable groups such as ACORN to partake in the counting. We must all demand that Congress and this administration count us properly, so our voices can be heard loud and clear. We will not allow this process to be used to further any agenda but what was intended to protect our right to equal representation. I believe that we must protest this injustice by calling on all of government, including the Supreme Court, and all of our nationally elected officials to abide by their oath of office and ensure that our rights as citizens are not diluted by artificial numbers.

I urge you to become involved, to write, e-mail, call, or visit your representatives and senators. Voice your displeasure and question the validity of what the government intends to do. We must start petitions, assemble and march on our government offices, and inundate the media by any means necessary to get our message out before it is too late. Only through the strength of overwhelming numbers can the government be forced to change its direction in this crucial matter. Our federal government must be held accountable to fulfill their duties and uphold their oaths of office. Again to quote Thomas Jefferson, "All it takes for tyranny to gain a foothold is for people of good conscience to remain silent."[1]

Our candidates in the upcoming election must understand this issue and pledge to declare this census invalid. A new census must be called for and undertaken as soon as possible. Our candidates must also pledge to fulfill this constitutionally mandated responsibility as frugally and efficiently as possible. They must also pledge to put a system in place to ensure the census is done properly in the future as called for in the constitution.

We must heed the call of our Founding Fathers, who understood that freedom does not come free and every generation has a right and a responsibility to secure the blessings of liberty for ourselves and our descendants. Again, I can't stress enough what an enormous challenge we face in 2010 to ensure our republic stays true to our ideals and remains humanity's best hope for freedom and liberty in the world. We are the shining example the world has looked to for greatness and leadership from for centuries. We are the one country that will do whatever we can to champion the causes of liberty, human rights, and democracy for oppressed people throughout the world. Our sons and daughters have fought and died for centuries and continue to do so willingly to ensure that our way of life is secure for us all. The least we can do is raise our voices in unison to ensure that their sacrifices have not been in vain.

Notes

1. Thomas Jefferson. BrainyQuote.com, Xplore Inc, 2010. http://www.brainyquote.com/quotes/quotes/t/thomasjeff136431.html, accessed July25, 2010.

CHAPTER 7

Congressional Redistricting

Congressional redistricting is one of the most controversial and constitutionally questionable practices in modern-day politics. The redistricting is based on the results of the census, which is constitutionally mandated to occur once every ten years. The problem with the census as conducted today is that it does not meet its mandated function of counting only the citizens of voting age to determine congressional representation among the states.

The ideal number of members has been a hotly debated issue since the country's founding. George Washington felt that the original representation proposed in the Constitutional Convention, one representative for every forty thousand citizens, was inadequate and argued to increase that number to one representative for every thirty thousand. It would be the only time throughout the entire convention that Washington would give an opinion on any of the issues debated. He felt strongly enough about our rights to be represented adequately to speak out on this issue. The Constitution initially set the number at one representative per every thirty thousand citizens, influenced no doubt by George Washington's persuasion.

The size of the U.S. House of Representatives has since been capped at 435 voting members, representing an average of 650,000 people per district. I cannot disagree with the logic of capping the number of representatives, as the old saying goes, "Too many chefs spoil the broth." This common sense logic was first raised by James Madison, who said, "I take for granted here what I shall, in answering the forth objection, hereinafter show, that the number of representatives will be augmented from time to time in the manner provided by the Constitution. On a contrary supposition, I should admit the objection to have very great weight indeed. Sixty or seventy men may be more properly trusted with a given degree of power than six or seven. But it does not follow that six or seven hundred would be proportionably a better depositary. And if we carry on the supposition to six or seven thousand, the whole reasoning ought to be reversed. In all very numerous assemblies, of whatever character composed, passion never fails to wrest the sceptre from reason."[1] He argued against the assumption that more is better, understanding that the potential population growth of our nation could cause a situation where the numbers would be too great to govern effectively.

I believe this argument to be valid, as it is much harder to find consensus within a large group than it is among members of a smaller group. The issue is not one of how many representatives we have but more important, how the districts are drawn to give us a true representation of who we are as a people. This allows large groups of people to become disenfranchised from our political system, as they realize their votes are, in essence, wasted because of the racial or ethnic makeup of their district. We cannot allow this process to be used to give any group a disproportionate voice to the detriment of any other group. This practice of partisan politics using the process for their own political gain by packing districts with sufficient supporters to make it almost impossible for opposition candidates to win is all too prevalent in our current system and must be ended.

The problem with the redistricting process is that it is a partisan process in all but five states: Hawaii, Idaho, Montana, New Jersey, and Washington. All fifty states draw their districts with guidelines that include: the districts must be contiguous, continuously connected, they must keep districts compact, not splitting political subdivisions, while preserving communities of interest. There are twenty-four Democratically controlled states to only thirteen controlled by Republicans; the others are split. The immediate prize is federal money distributed on the basis of population, but also potential political control for the next ten years in some states.

We deserve a better system than what is in place. We need to hold our representatives accountable to doing all within their power to make the census bureau perform its constitutional responsibility to count the citizens eighteen years old and older, those of voting age as changed in the Twenty-Fourth Amendment, which lowered it from twenty-one, as originally written in Article 1 Section 2. Additional counting can be done to determine equitable distribution of federal funds for services for children and the elderly, whether citizens or legal residents. Illegal immigrants need to be denied funding, because they are criminals by virtue of breaking our immigration laws.

The census bureau must do an accurate count of citizens first so our votes can be meaningfully counted and equally distributed among the states. Additionally, all congressional districts must be created through bipartisan groups that are of equal composition as prescribed by state law. The judicial branch will ultimately be given the primary responsibility to ensure our constitutionally ensured rights are protected if the plans do not adequately protect us and our right to have our votes count.

This is an area where state constitutions can be amended if necessary to ensure that all fifty states create an equally split bipartisan commission that draws the new congressional districts according to a state-certified census. This is where the states must band together to hold the federal government accountable for providing an accurate census that is fair and equitable to all the states. They must ensure the census equally distributes not only congressional seats by states' citizens of voting age but also Electoral College votes as the balance of power changes as some states gain or lose representatives.

The states may sue the federal government for not carrying out the constitutional mandate of counting citizens of voting age to apportion the House of Representatives. The judicial branch must then declare the 2010 census invalid and, therefore, null and void. However the census can be overturned, it must be done. Call your U.S. Census Bureau and ask them how they verify American citizenship, and they will tell you they don't ask. Now, I ask you to consider by what measure do we complete redistricting? Our candidates at the state and federal levels must pledge to scrap the 2010 census and begin a proper counting to complete the appointed task, so the House of Representatives is truly representative of our citizenry and our Electoral College is accurate for our next presidential election in 2012.

Notes

1. James Madison, The Federalist no. 55, a letter to the people of New York,Wednesday, February 13, 1788
http://www.constitution.org/fed/federa55.htm, accessed March 25, 2010.

CHAPTER 8

Sunshine Laws

This is an issue that we must not only speak out vocally through peaceful assembly, e-mails, phone calls, and all means available to us to keep our representatives honest to the promises they make to us as candidates. We must also seek redress through legal means for any legislation without authors who write it, show it to us, and then debate it for all to see as in the health care reform bill debacle. How our representatives and senators could cast a vote for something they hadn't had the chance to read in its entirety seems ludicrous. No longer can we allow our politicians to craft a bill of any size, let alone one that has enormous impact on all of us and our future. We need stronger laws in all fifty states and the District of Columbia. They are required to ensure the public that our laws are not only crafted for the greater good, as we the people decide, but are done with dignity, honor, and constitutionally legal methods.

The recent health-care reform bill was unethical, immoral, and unconstitutional. The Constitution gives Congress the power to raise taxes as needed but with the caveat that the taxes must be distributed evenly among all the states. The deal worked out in the Senate, in which Senator Nelson of Nebraska's vote was bought with language exempting his state from Medicare cost increases in perpetuity, is illegal. In other words, other states will have to split the burden of paying Nebraska's fair share of the cost of the bill, which, in the language above, is clearly at odds with Congress's authority as spelled out in the Constitution in Article 1, Section 8. The deal offered to Senator Landrieu, in which her district received $3,000,000 in exchange for her vote, is yet another example of a politician ignoring the greater national interest to pander to her constituents. She has stated she is unapologetic for the agreement.

Once again, we would never see this type of deal occur if we were allowed to watch the proceedings and debates. We would be outraged, and rightfully so, if a bill were truly in our best interest shady deals would be unnecessary to acquire the votes needed. The fact that a nationally elected official would put the country's interests in peril for political gain is reason enough for us to end the practice of politics as usual. None of this would have been possible under public scrutiny. We must demand that our politicians cast their votes in the national interest. They must debate openly and honestly in the light of public view, so we may know that our interests, opinions, and laws are being followed for the betterment of our great nation.

We must hold our candidates for office in 2010 to pledge to outlaw these practices and make sunshine laws a part of our legislative process at all levels of government. To do less—except in cases of national security, where secrecy is required to keep us safe from our enemies— takes us down a perilous path. Our Founding Fathers knew this to be true. They knew our very liberties could be lost if we were not vigilante. To quote Patrick Henry, "The liberties of a people never were, nor ever will be, secure, when the transactions of their rulers may be concealed from them."[1] This is not government for the people, by the people as our Founding Fathers so eloquently wrote when they wrote our divinely inspired Declaration of Independence and the Constitution of the United States. The media should be used to air proceedings in either the House or Senate, especially those that are momentous and affect not only us but our future generations as well.

Notes

Patrick Henry. BrainyQuote.com, Xplore Inc, 2010. http://www. brainyquote.com/quotes/quotes/p/patrickhen143315.html, accessed May 21, 2010.

CHAPTER 9

Legislation in Plain Language

The Constitution's Preamble expresses our reasons for the creation of a federal government, its sole purposes, the scope and limitations of its power, and where it is derived from: we, the people. It clearly states that we by consent give limited areas of responsibility to the federal government above the states, article-by-article and section-by-section. We here also affirm our unalienable rights and guaranteed freedoms, which have made us the envy of the world.

Here, we have another obvious need for our candidates to make a pledge if they expect our support and votes. All proposed bills and amendments must be written in concise, clear, plain language. Make it clear what the rationale is, tell us why we need this now, tell us what it will cost, and how it will, according to the Constitution, "establish Justice, insure domestic Tranquility, provide for the common defense, promote the general Welfare, and secure the Blessings of Liberty to ourselves and our Posterity."

We need bills written that clearly state how they apply to and improve on an area of the federal government's five areas of responsibility as written in our Constitution, while securing our defined liberties. This is extremely simple, as all of our elected officials should be well versed in what they swear to perpetuate: "This Constitution, and the Laws of the United States which shall be made in Pursuance thereof; and all Treaties made, or which shall be made, under the Authority of the United States, shall be the supreme Law of the Land; and the Judges in every State shall be bound thereby, any Thing in the Constitution or Laws of any State to the Contrary notwithstanding." That again tells the federal government they are not empowered beyond the Constitution, for it is the supreme law of the land. They must also define exactly what the benefit is and who, if anyone benefits disproportionately. There must be a projected cost of the bill, and it must state who is responsible to pay for it.

There is no reason for our elected officials to write legislation in terms incomprehensible to the common man and woman. No longer should a bill be written in legal terms and excessive length to hide the true intentions and consequences of the proposed legislation from the people. All bills must be written in this manner and available for the public to read and express our opinions to our elected officials so that they may vote in the interests of the people they serve. Again, I need to express clearly that we, the citizenry of this country, must examine these bills and ensure we believe they are in line with our national values and common interests. No longer can we expect or encourage our elected officials to vote for earmarks, special projects that benefit one group or area, without advancing the common good. This is especially true now, as we face the most massive budget deficit in our history.

Congress has a duty to conduct its business in a manner that is clear, transparent, and readily available for perusal by the media and the citizens. We must be given time to review proposed legislation and inject our voices into the debates, and we can only do that if we have the ability to know what exactly is at stake. The media's role as an independent entity, free of government control, is essential here to keep the people of this great nation informed about the workings of our government, especially in terms of how it affects the free market principle on which this country was founded, how our freedoms and financial burden in these tough economic times will be impacted, and what the proposed solutions to our present problems and vulnerabilities are doing or will do on our behalf.

The length of a proposed bill should also be shortened by the use of plain language. There is no need to use legal terms and language, since all we need to know is if the terms of the law are legal according to the Constitution. The debate should be straightforward and, therefore, again short, unless the minority party has just cause to make use of the filibuster in the Senate, where it takes sixty votes to end debate on proposed legislation. This strategy, of course, can't be used indiscriminately but must be used in scenarios where the minority interest is in line with the will of the people, and the Congress and president are controlled by the same party, as it is currently.

So, we must end the way bills are prepared, the language used, the time we are given as a people to review and make our voices heard, and hold our government accountable to fulfilling their duties as public servants. We need to be able to watch and influence the debates as they unfold. This, unfortunately, is what our times have come to: the need for citizens to be vigilant about what is being done, supposedly on our behalf. Demand changes in the way our politics is conducted not only in Washington, D.C., but at all levels of government—from local elections for school boards that dictate what our children's future could very possibly be and to every elected official across this land. We must demand and expect no less for the future of our republic, our system of government and the very light of freedom for the world hangs in the balance.

Every generation has its challenges and opportunities. This is our moment of truth. This is the moment history has presented to us and by which we will be judged. To wrest control of our government from the special interests and corruption, which permeates almost all levels of government. To repudiate policies and decisions that threaten our national security. Outside of the massive debt that we have incurred to foreign powers, not exactly with our interests in mind, we'd be wise to try and amend this dangerous course. We must also ensure that our enemies are identified and treated appropriately. To the majority of Americans, I believe the people understand the prosecution of the war on terrorism as our righteous response to an act of war and should be treated as such. There can be no civilian trials for terrorists, especially in our cities. We should not grant these enemy combatants our rights as citizens, which they have sworn to destroy even at the cost of their own lives. We must use all the strength, might, technology, and common sense of our vast intelligence- gathering operations and military assets to protect America and its allies. Any less threatens our way of life and the best hope for a world controlled by limited government interference, maximum personal liberty, and the principles of our Founding Fathers, who sought God's blessings on the behalf of all humanity.

CHAPTER 10

Government Lobbying

The need for lobbying our leaders is an extension of our freedom of speech rights. This, I believe, was reflected in the recent Supreme Court decision in *Citizens United vs. Federal Election Commission*. Lobbying is not necessarily a dirty word though it is often associated with corruption, undue influence of money, and the power of money to influence and even sway elections. I believe in our freedom of speech, and attempts to limit it impacts our ability to speak as a group for whatever cause we choose to embrace and seek to influence for the good of all. Consider, for example, the common benefit to all of society of ending life altering or fatal illnesses as an example. Illnesses such as cancer, diabetes, muscular sclerosis to name just a few if eradicated would save the nation money for care and enable the individuals to contribute to society to their full potential. How can we dismiss groups that seek to find cures for those who suffer and could add so much to our country should they regain their ability and health?

Lobbying needs to be strictly controlled, and this also speaks to our ability to ensure that no money but that from individual citizen donors, with limitations that equalize the field for ordinary citizens to finance campaigns, be made available. This will, of course, drastically lower the price of running campaigns, and I honestly can't see how that is contrary to the public good. Remember that large groups have the ability to buy valuable airtime to run commercials advocating their positions. Here again, we must decide if positions advocated by groups are in the common good, such as advocacy groups with nonpartisan agendas. Partisan ads should be clearly announced as to who they endorse.

We must also ensure that no money, gift, or type of function such as a party where gifts could be given serves as a means for our public servants to profit in any way. Public servants must be unable to profit personally or gain an edge against all potential or real challengers. Again, incumbency should not give an incumbent any financial advantage they can spend on election or primary elections. They can and should, of course, gain through their proven actions on our behalf in our national, state, or local interests, in the perspectives of cost, fiscal responsibility, and benefit to be gained. There should be a full accounting of anyone who may disproportionately be burdened or enhanced. Their efforts on our behalf should result in their reelection or by removing them from office short of reaching term-limit restrictions.

Once again, the duty here given us by our supreme law, the Constitution, is clear: to ensure that our interests come first and they are shown to be the proven priorities by the actions of our elected officials, who must remember they are our public servants. They work for us, the citizens of the United States of America, and we expect them to limit government intrusion, maximize our individual liberties, and to promote the ideals of a free market society based on capitalism.

We expect lobbying to be limited to discussion and access to our representatives on a level equal to our access to speak to them on the issues and legislative proposals. Our voices must be considered first, before those of special interests. Through the elimination of possible political or personal gain from lobbyists, our voices become clearly heard, and it becomes politically expedient in keeping or advancing their positions for them to listen to us. Holding them accountable is not only our God-given right but our civic duty to retain the republic our Founding Fathers gave us.

Lobbyists must be closely monitored, as should our elected officials' actions and their campaign fund-raising activities. Lobbying with its threat of corruption and, therefore, counter to our common interests must be controlled through elimination of groups' ability to raise funds or in any way solicit and deliver funds, manpower, or other material support to our candidates. This is not meant to infringe on free speech. To the contrary, it gives our individual voices the power we deserve.

This must be protected to keep the ballot box free from the possible corruption of powerful interests with financial power that could unduly influence our political process. They will be able to use the media to advance their causes. It is up to us, the American people, to make informed decisions on the issues we face. We must also be wary of false promises; again, we must refer to our common sense. There is another old saying that applies here, "If it sounds too good to be true, it probably is." How many of us have received e-mails telling us we have won millions of dollars in a lottery we did not enter or even heard of. All they ask for is some private information for verification purposes. The majority of us simply delete these e-mails, knowing the promises could not be true. We must use this same logic when we listen to political advertisements and our political candidates' positions on the important issues that affect us and are of utmost importance to us. We must hold our candidates and elected officials to keeping their promises or risk losing their positions, because we will hold them accountable at the ballot box.

CHAPTER 11

Defense and Homeland Security

The Constitution's Preamble gives the federal government authority to, "provide for the common defense." We live in precarious times, with real and potential adversaries from around the globe. Our candidates must understand their responsibility to keep us safe as we approach the ten-year anniversary of the destruction of the World Trade Center and the attack on the Pentagon, while another attacker was courageously destroyed by the sacrifice of American passengers who gave their lives to thwart further damage to our grateful nation. Still, to this day, the fact that those responsible have remained free and nothing has been built where the twin towers stood has left a scar that never heals. This hole in the heart of New York City should be a never-ending reminder of what we are facing. We cannot forget that in 1993, almost twenty years ago, the same group, al-Qaida tried blowing up the Twin Towers with a car bomb below the North Tower. Their intention was to knock the towers into each other and bring them both down. The plan's financier was Khalid Shaikh Mohammed; the results were the deaths of six people and the injury of 1,042 innocent people. Homeland Security will be discussed later, as we now must concentrate on national security, the defense piece.

America faces enemies of all types, as well as potential enemies who pose grave risks to our nation. We must act boldly through diplomacy as well as use our ability to protect our allies with our military might and capability. We need to define our present-day enemies to the world, namely extremist Islamic terrorists intent on establishing a worldwide caliphate. This includes the countries where they reside or those that give aid and arms to terrorists. This falls under the Bush doctrine, where we reserved the right to defend ourselves not only against attack but also through the right to carry out preemptive strikes against those who would do us harm. We must also make the world understand the threat they pose to Western and Eastern Europe as well as Asia. The world must stand up to those who seek to enslave or kill all who stand in their way. China, Russia, and the United States must put aside their differences and realize we face a common enemy to freedom, sovereignty, willing to kill all who would oppose their vision of religious oppression.

Our first area of attention must be Pakistan and Afghanistan, where our military must confront and defeat the Taliban and al-Qaida. This fight has been not fully fought and should never have been allowed to take this long. Going forward, American, coalition, and NATO forces under our command must openly formalize our alliance to defend Pakistan against our common foes; this must be made clear to all. We should be working with Pakistan's military and intelligence forces to secure its government, starting in the lawless tribal lands, until together we destroy, defeat, and eradicate them completely. This includes killing or capturing Osama bin Laden and his second in command, Ayman Al-Zawahiri, and the Taliban leadership.

Pakistan is the new frontline in the war on terror, which actually began in 1993, with the first attempt to blow up the Trade Centers. Some of us believe that September 11, 2001, was it, the beginning of World War III; others have yet to acknowledge that it is. Sadly, the intention of these enemies of freedom to annihilate the entire world must be faced now with the full capabilities of our military assets. The countries of the world must acknowledge and shoulder their portion of the burden to save our collective sovereignty. Pakistan is a nation with nuclear arms that can't be allowed to fall into the hands of our enemies. The Pakistanis, and indeed the world, must understand that failure here would lead to us having no choice but to destroy their nuclear forces preemptively by any means necessary. Our common interest and that of the entire Western world, as well as all non-Muslim civilizations, is clear here, as even our potential enemies and allies all face Islamic radical unrest and violence. The reason for what we must do was eloquently spoken before, ironically during World War II, as part of a radio address on December 9, 1941 by Franklin D. Roosevelt: "We are now in the midst of a war, not for conquest, not for vengeance, but for a world in which this nation, and all that this nation represents, will be safe for our children. We expect to eliminate the danger from Japan, but it would serve us ill if we accomplished that and found that the rest of the world was dominated by Hitler and Mussolini. So we are going to win the war and we are going to win the peace that follows."[1]

Our troops can be drawn down from Europe, Iraq, and parts of Asia, as we begin to force our allies to face the financial burden of securing their freedom. We and our allies have to understand and act on the fact that this is World War III. The Japanese, Europeans, and the rest of the world need to contribute troops, resources, and to pay their share of the costs involved in securing of peace and prosperity we have made possible for more than sixty-five years. We need to begin to seek financial reimbursement for our deployments of troops abroad, while also promoting the growth of our allies' capabilities to defend themselves adequately. There is one thing we manufacture without equal, and that is military equipment. Arm sales, especially of missile defense and aircraft systems, can be good for the American, economy as we create jobs in the private sector. The sale of our equipment, coupled with the cost of deploying our troops to secure and use our material in places like the Middle East and Eastern Europe, will allow us to fund our military while cutting costs for the American people who have ensured freedom for generations of people throughout the world. We will continue our preeminence in continuing this proud tradition. Our allies will clearly see and follow our leadership, and this will reestablish our place as the benevolent superpower to be respected and unchallenged by any that feel emboldened to think us weakened or unable to continue to lead the free world. Asking our allies in Germany and Japan alone to provide the equivalent of half the forces currently deployed in troops and resources or pay the price of the cost would add fifty thousand troops and materials to help win the war in Pakistan and Afghanistan.[2] In other countries with al-Qaida ties, including Yemen and Somalia, al-Qaida would be weakened and ripe for taking down by governments willing to do their part with international assistance.

These people would be brought to justice using their full capabilities and the assistance of American technology.

The other imminent threat is from Iran, whose rocket, missile, and nuclear weapons capabilities cannot be tolerated. We and our allies need to destroy their military capabilities and free their people, who clearly yearn for freedom from oppression. This could be seen by the pictures of civil unrest following the last presidential election. The aim here is not to occupy the country, as we can reach out across the world for peacekeepers to free us up. We must not repeat the mistake of Iraq, where we won the war but lost the peace. The war to topple the government took approximately three weeks and our troops were generally received as liberators.

Greed on our nation's part that precluded those governments that objected to the war but sought to cash in on the opportunity to seek to profit from reconstruction of a war-torn country was a huge mistake. International bidding would have freed up our money, the stipulation being the contribution of peacekeeping troops in areas of no strategic value to U.S. national security. It would have freed us to leave as liberators and also would have muted international opposition to the war. I believe our media, specifically those involved in the airing of the piece on Abu Gharib on *60 Minutes*, should be tried for treason. In the beginning, we were perceived as liberators, which was our intention. The story on *60 Minutes* depicting us as torturing and humiliating the inmates hurt our moral standing and credibility. To the Muslim world particularly we became to be viewed as disrespectful occupiers who perpetrated cruelty we were supposed to be freeing them from. This became a rallying cry for the insurgency. Their actions aided and abetted our enemies and unnecessarily endangered our troops. Our moral standing was weakened in the eyes of the world, and years of conflict and injuries were added, which could have been avoided. Had Iraq been successfully stabilized, Iran could have been the next to experience regime change, as obviously desired based on its people's actions. All of this would have been in the civilized world's best interests. The coming together of countries with a common purpose could have led to a better future for us all.

A stable Iraq with a majority Shiite population, with a majority government with diverse ethnic and religious groups governing together in peace, would have been ideally suited to provide peacekeeping troops with the overthrow of the present terrorist-sponsoring regime in Iran since both countries are predominantly Shiite. Our Arab allies would have been freed from the specter of the threat from non-Arab, Persian Iran, which it now poses to them, and there would be a free flowing of oil through the Persian Gulf. This being their economic lifeline and only valuable commodity, it is imperative to them and the world that the uninterrupted flow of commerce through this strategic waterway be ensured. They would be indebted to us for freeing them from a danger to their survival. Iran and their growing missile and nuclear capabilities also threaten our troops in Europe and Asia, as well as many allies, including Israel. Russia also faces the threat, and working together with us could have furthered peace and goodwill.

China also must be engaged, as they face the same problems we all do: a fanaticism that cannot be reasoned with and, therefore, must be destroyed. Russia, China, and all who face this threat must join together in plain-talk diplomacy to end it now. These times require the world's nations to realize what is at stake for all. This must be the moment America again leads with morality to destroy a cancer to civilization and our ideals.

The war—once won with the defeat and dismantling of the Taliban, al-Qaida, and the overthrow of the repressive Islamic clerics of Iran— would change the balance of power in the Middle East. Hamas and Hezbollah would be irreparably harmed, and their undue influence would end in rogue nations such as Syria, Lebanon, and Jordan. They would acknowledge the only problem is between the Palestinians and Israelis and none of their business. It is an issue that goes back thousands of years, and in an environment of peace, it could finally be resolved. Arab nations must understand and accept that the so-called, "right of return" issue where displaced Palestinians return to their former homes inside Israel is impossible for the Israelis to accept, and the responsibility of the Arab League is to help their displaced brethren. Especially oil-rich Gulf states, such as Saudi Arabia, if they see this as a moral issue, should lead the way in offering assistance to all of the Palestinian people. Saudi Arabia must also end the status quo of not confronting the radical extremism of Wahhabism to ensure their monarchy's political power.

There are also real enemies in Venezuela, where Hugo Chavez is a virulent anti-American and a genuine threat to peace. His alliances with Cuba and Russia, culminating in the passage of the first Russian naval vessel through the Panama Canal since 1944 after conducting joint naval exercises with the Venezuelan Navy, is an example of unacceptable meddling in our sphere of influence. It is also in direct defiance of our Monroe Doctrine. The Russians have also sold large quantities of arms to Venezuela, which has also sought ties with Iran. Venezuela is an enemy in our own backyard. We've claimed this to be our area of influence, not subject to foreign meddling, since the Monroe Doctrine in 1823. The Russians and Iranians must be kept out of our hemisphere. We cannot allow them to be emboldening or arming our enemies. Here we must stand by the Monroe Doctrine and end the possibility of threats to us by foreign powers who aid our enemies in our backyard.

Another country we must continue to be vigilant of is North Korea. They must dismantle their nuclear program under strict verifiable observation, and all nuclear material secured. China can be especially valuable if they choose to be. A nuclear-free Korean Peninsula is in everyone's best interest, especially China's. They do not want to see nuclear missiles deployed so close to their country. China also would be freed from subsidizing a failed economy by endorsing unification. The two nations need to take time to work together to see it is in their best interest. Though the disparity will be quite a challenge to overcome considering the poverty in North Korea, together they can find a path to peace and prosperity. This changes worthless subsidization into an opportunity for a new, emerging market in the global marketplace. This could drastically cut our troop deployment and associated costs, as the Korean War, which ended in a truce with a heavily armed border, could conclude with a peace treaty. The people of Korea, who we have helped defend for over fifty years, would finally realize their dream of reunification with loved ones on both sides of the border.

These are the threats and active enemies that, if we are able to agree the threat they pose is universal, we can eliminate by uniting with other countries such as Russia and China to face our common foes. The ability to forge new relationships could turn potential adversaries into allies. However, if it does not happen, we must be prepared to face the challenges of the twenty-first century and continue to be the beacon of freedom to all around the world. This includes Russia and China, which are, once again, seeking to surpass us when we are perceived as down and weakened. Russia has unveiled a stealth fighter designed to rival the U.S. F-22 Raptor, the premier operational plane in the world. Remember, the current administration, in an attempt to appease and win favor with the Russians, scrapped a planned deployment of missile defense systems in Poland. To this point, the Russians have made every effort to thumb their noses at us. Their actions point to a continued effort to challenge us on the world stage for supremacy.

China also looks to surpass us as the next global leader. Their military has sought the ability to destroy satellites and did shoot one of their own down. They have been pursuing capabilities in space, understanding the importance and abilities they can add not only to them but also to potential adversaries, namely us. China is such a populous nation that it has well positioned itself as a tough competitor on the world stage in every arena. It has a large military with nuclear capabilities.

China has kept its currency undervalued and left their people in poverty. It has, however, learned from Hong Kong and allowed limited capitalism to begin to lead them to great wealth and the potential to be an economic powerhouse for years to come. Their people are a workforce with no rights or education, but they can use them to produce a growing economy and further influence in the world. China will be competing with us for resources, as their needs grow and as they produce more products for export at prices kept artificially low. This gives them an unfair edge, as they sell all types of products, from toys to electronics. They hold massive amounts of our debt currently estimated to be 867.7 billion dollars, which they have used as leverage.[3] They have used it to intimidate the current administration into stopping the investigation of their spies. This, while they launch cyber-attacks against us, constantly try to evade our defenses, and practice espionage to close the technology gap between us. We need to build our defenses and attack their capabilities in kind to show our resolve and make them reconsider this type of provocation.

The huge amount of threats we face, coupled with the potential and real enemies we have, means we must show that our resolve and strength will prevent us from being defeated. We must also show our ability to use diplomacy to gain other nations' help and understanding. We are not looking to occupy or expand our reach. We are merely stating our objectives and expectations of the world to rid it of a real, determined, and evil group that seeks to conquer or destroy all who would oppose their vision of the world.

Homeland security is a complex matter itself. We, as a people, need to be vigilant to the possibility of abuse of our individual liberties. Again, I believe it to be a matter of common sense. That part of the equation is best begun with the words of our Founding Fathers to consider the possible danger to our liberty. First, the words of Ben Franklin, who said, "Those who would give up essential liberty to purchase a little temporary safety, deserve neither liberty or safety."[4] John Adams warned, "A Constitution of Government once changed from freedom can never be restored. Liberty once lost, is lost forever."[5] The war we are now waging is a challenge, because our enemies' tactics violate the rules of war the world has known and followed to this point.

I believe it is important to differentiate between American citizens and enemy combatants. We retain all of our rights through the Constitution's Bill of Rights. Enemy combatants have no rights under our Constitution. Those captured should be transferred immediately to military facilities to be tried in military tribunals with no recourse. Our rights are not theirs; our court systems do not apply to these people. These people operate not dressed in uniform of a country or group of countries they represent, and they target civilians. No country claims responsibility, or they offer official public support of their actions. The supporters of Islamic terrorists may claim innocence, but they are certainly not. This leaves these people outside of the Geneva Convention, as they are not covered. They breach the limits of warfare through their actions or intentions and are not prisoners of war. Intelligence attained by all lawful means must be gathered, disseminated, analyzed, and used to our maximum advantage.

The current administration has failed us by not holding anyone accountable. Homeland Security Secretary Janet Napolitano even went so far as to publicly announce, "The system worked," in the case of the Christmas Day bomber, foiled by a Norwegian passenger who stopped a Nigerian man. We had been warned by the father that this man had become radicalized. Should we not question her fitness to lead? That statement showed us a person being clueless in an important post, and she should have been fired or resigned. Given the facts in hand, the system failed miserably, and even the president had to acknowledge the failure. He has not helped to explain her statements and has done nothing within his assembled team. He immediately ruled out terrorist ties in this attack and the one at Fort Hood, though it seems apparent that the government knew of Major Nidal Hassan's views and foreign radical associates but again did nothing. The attack carried out on the largest U.S. Army base in the world by one man leaving so much devastation in his wake is unpardonable in light of what they knew about this man. The fact that army personnel felt they shouldn't say anything in the current political climate speaks volumes about this administration and its policies. Despite what we've learned and seen since September 11, 2001, there appears to be a wealth of pre-9/11 thinking, which is clearly naive, ignorant, and dangerous. The government's handling of these events shows a failure of its ability to provide for the common defense, its constitutionally mandated area of responsibility.

I believe most would agree that if e-mails are being sent to and from foreign entities or individuals known to be active in jihad against us, the government should be looking at what's going on. It's no different than if law enforcement agencies become aware of affiliations with known criminal organizations. We must review how we handle the difference between legal statuses of citizens, legal immigrants, residents, and illegal immigrants, including overstaying visas. Our rights as citizens are guaranteed by the Constitution; the others must depend on their status as well as the circumstances in which they are charged and captured. The much-maligned Patriot Act, with its need for reauthorization into law, is wise, as it allows us to review as a people whether the threat remains sufficient to justify the measures allowed or if they should be suspended or ended.

Our candidates must be strong on national defense and ready to wage the war in homeland defense with common sense, using all of our capabilities to gather actionable intelligence and shorten this war by disrupting their actions, thus helping in the dismantling and destruction of al-Qaida as a military force. Theirs is an ideology that threatens all nations, and we must lead with boldness and with candidness with both our allies and adversaries. We must articulate our intentions clearly as a nation and not seek to conquer and expand our reach, with troops occupying foreign soil. We simply seek out those who have done us so much harm and threaten our way of life until they are eradicated once and for all.

Candidates must also pledge to fulfill their oath to the Constitution to continue to defend all Americans' constitutionally protected rights. It is a balancing act. I do not feel it is simply black and white but many areas of gray. It is clear, however, that our rights must be protected at all costs, or we have lost the war by losing who we are as a people in our traditions, values, and laws. We must remain true to who we are and remember what has led to our ability to become the guardians of freedom when the world is faced with great peril. It has always been our destiny to follow our traditional values and vanquish evil. This is our generation's fight: to win yet remain Americans, true to our values and principles, continuing our heritage as the envy of the world. This is our calling, which cannot be ignored if we are to continue to be the America we have always been, an unmatched power for good in the world.

Notes

1. Franklin Roosevelt radio address, December 9, 1941
http://www.mhric.org/fdr/chat19.html, accessed March 25, 2010

2. world wide military deployment http://www.globalsecurity.org/
military/world/deploy.htm, accessed December 22, 2009

3. Foreign holders of U.S. debt, U.S. Treasury report
http://www.ustreas.gov/tic/mfh.txt, accessed July 31, 2010

4. Ben Franklin, Historical Review of Pennsylvania, 1759
http://www.quotationspage.com/quotes/Benjamin_Franklin/31,
accessed July 31, 2010

5. John Adams letter to Abigail Adams, July 17, 1775
http://johnadamsweb.com/adamsquotes.html, accessed July 31, 2010

Chapter 12

Balanced Budgets

The U.S. government budget for 2011 is 3.8 trillion dollars and is projected to triple the national debt. This, at a time when our debt ceiling has continued to be raised to historical highs in the midst of a severe economic downturn and high unemployment, is ludicrous and puts us all in jeopardy. We have witnessed double-digit unemployment and watched our gross domestic product (GDP) drop drastically. This is a recipe for disaster and a road we must straighten out immediately. We can't continue to allow our foreign debt to increase. In the words of Ben Franklin, "The borrower is a slave to the lender, and the debtor to the creditor."[1] Much of our debt and many of our imports are from nations that are not allies but adversaries. This threat to our sovereignty is intolerable and must be rectified now.

Many Americans have sadly learned this lesson the hard way in their own personal lives. The stock market crash cost people approximately half of their retirement funds, hurting those who were near retiring the most. Americans also watched as the value of their homes dropped to less than half their prior worth. Americans were left with upside-down mortgages, loans for more than the houses are worth. This robbed them of equity and made it extremely difficult to move without losing enormous amounts of money.

The American people have lost much but have also learned much. We must live within our means, personally and as a nation, and cut back wherever we can to lower our debt and increase our savings. We can't continue to spend more year after year when we make less and have less, and not expect to find ourselves unable to care for our families. It is time for America to search our hearts and ask ourselves what we truly believe is the role of the federal government. Do we wish to buy things we can't afford? Do we expect the government to be large and empowered beyond its constitutional scope, to care for us whatever the cost, or to be limited as required by our Constitution and involved only in the areas our Founding Fathers saw common need and justification?

To spend ourselves into a debt we can never repay if we continue this increased deficit puts our liberties at risk. We, as a debtor nation, will have little choice. A large government caring for us, especially at this cost with our debt situation, is not what our Founding Fathers wished for but feared. John Adams had a few thoughts that I believe deserve our consideration. First, "If ye love wealth better than liberty, the tranquility of servitude than the animating contest of freedom, go from us in peace. We ask not your counsels or arms, crouch down and lick the hands which feed you. May your chains sit lightly upon you and may posterity forget that ye were our countrymen!"[2] The danger here is of democracy falling as a result of decadence. To again quote our first vice president and second president, "Democracy never lasts long. It soon wastes, exhausts and murders itself. There was never a democracy that did not commit suicide."[3]

I believe most Americans understand this valuable lesson and embrace the value of liberty. The threat of debt demands that our political representatives reflect our views and respect our wishes. This is where we must enact legislation to force Congress to pass balanced budgets through a major downsizing of the government bureaucracy. The government must run lean in hard times, just as successful companies do to weather the hard times, and we must position ourselves to gear up quickly to becoming prosperous again.

We must be productive through tax breaks and incentives for business to invest in America and her workforce, which is the envy of the world. Job creation through the private sector is historically what America has done best and needs to do now. We must regain our edge in the ability to compete on the global stage with innovation and productivity to keep our prices competitive. We can't be successful as a debtor country. It is morally incomprehensible to leave our children with a debt to pay on our behalf. Thomas Jefferson said, "Then I say, the earth belongs to each of these generations during its course, fully and in its own right. The second generation receives it clear of the debts and encumbrances of the first, the third of the second and so on."[4] We must get our economy moving and our debt reduced, not increased. Balanced budgets are the least we can do.

We owe our children, grandchildren, and posterity all the liberties we have claimed for ourselves from the Creator and have constitutionally protected since the founding of the republic with the enactment the U.S. Constitution. Ronald Reagan, the fortieth president, said, "We have once again reminded the people that man is not free unless government is limited. There is clear cause and effect there that is neat and predictable as a law of physics. As government expands liberty contracts."[5] We owe it to our children and the world to act now, before it is too late.

Notes

1. Ben Franklin, *The Way to Wealth*
http://itech.fgcu.edu/faculty/wohlpart/alra/franklin.htm#Way, accessed July 31, 2010.

2. John Adams, in a letter written after the Battle of Lexington
http://www.americanchristianhistory.com/christianhistory10.html, accessed July 31, 2010.

3. John Adams, in a letter written April 15, 1814
http://www.quotationspage.com/quote/27459.html, accessed July 31, 2010.

4. Thomas Jefferson letter to John Adams, September 6, 1789
http://press-pubs.uchicago.edu/founders/print_documents/v1ch2s23.html, accessed July 31, 2010.

5. Ronald Reagan Farewell address
http://www.reaganlibrary.net/, accessed July 31, 2010.

CHAPTER 13

Foreign Aid Budget

The foreign aid budget is a component of the overall budget, so it must be viewed in value versus need and cost. It deserves special scrutiny as to why the foreign aid is in our national interest. In matters of war and homeland security, we expect nothing less than complete victory. Yet, we have not fully used our complete capabilities to prosecute this war against those who attacked us.

In the face of a recession and a growing deficit, the Obama administration doubled the foreign aid budget in their first year to over $50 billion dollars. America's people have a history of generosity and will always respond to disasters, such as the recent earthquakes in Haiti and Chile. The foreign aid budget must be carefully reviewed to ensure they are necessary to our national interests. This is not to say that our history of generosity should be forgotten. However, as we continue to run up huge amounts of debt, we can't give away what we don't have. The American people have always responded charitably to people in need wherever they may be.

Matters of national security should be our major focus. Aid may also come in the way of training, jet fighters, and weaponry of all types from American military defense contractors. Troops could be deployed to different countries with anything from drones, missile interceptor batteries, and radar stations. This could help stimulate our economy, as jobs are created to meet increased demand. Our allies, whose freedom we have fought and died for twice and asked for nothing in return, must now do their part. Through programs such as the Lend-Lease Act and Marshall Plan, we have used our generosity to free and rebuild our allies, and enemies as well. The Lend-Lease Act passed on March 8, 1941 allowed us to arm England and any other country deemed important to our national security. The Soviet Union and China also received significant aid through this law. The Marshall Plan as it was known came into effect on April 3, 1948 when President Truman signed the European Recovery Plan. The plan was in effect for three years and cost the United States $12,500.000.00. The result was European manufacturing was brought back to thirty percent above their prewar levels.

Europe should remember this well, as well as our ability to ensure their freedom when a new potential adversary became evident. They must now shoulder more of their own defense and assist in the wars in Pakistan and Afghanistan to defeat and destroy al-Qaida and the Taliban. NATO must send their fair share of troops and materials to destroy or capture its fighters, sympathizers, and leadership. The NATO alliance has long protected Western Europe through our generosity. It is their turn to realize the premise has not changed; the enemy has shifted. We still face a common enemy.

Our foreign aid budget needs to be reviewed while the government seeks increased help from our allies. We must also review some of our current commitments to international bodies, such as the United Nations. We are currently responsible for twenty-two percent of its annual budget that comes to $1,080, 00,000. This is ridiculous and doesn't count peacekeeping operations which the U.S. pays at a higher percentage, currently 26 percent at a cost to American taxpayers of an additional $2.1 billion dollars. The top 17 countries pay 85.6 percent of the budget while the lowest 128 pay only 1 percent.[1] One nation one vote in the General Assembly: why should we subsidize the world at this rate, while we house the body in New York City? The United Nations began with 51 members in 1945 and has since ballooned to 192 with the addition of Montenegro in 2006. All of our foreign aid should be looked at in this light. Is it fair to the American taxpayer and in our national interests?

This applies to all commitments to all international institutions. We must ensure our aid is necessary and not going to those who don't need it. We must not subsidize any disarmament agreement with Russia to secure their nuclear materials. Let them be equal partners if they choose to be; we will no longer pay them for doing what we both see as in our mutual interests. America can no longer afford to pay to assist foes and potential adversaries, as all nations begin looking to supplant us and take away our position as the preeminent power and benevolent benefactor to all who would emulate our position as guarantor of freedom and liberty throughout the world.

Notes

1. UN Budget
http://www.foxnews.com/world/2009/09/17/budget-believe-billion/,
accessed July 31, 2010.

CHAPTER 14

Education

There is no doubt that our global ability to compete depends on the education of the next generation. The importance of education to the future of this country and our children is undeniable. Giving them the skills to reach their potential ability should be our goal. They must be strong in all academic areas, including math, science, reading, writing, and especially history. The concepts of the American Revolution that led to our founding and the republican form of government as spelled out in our Constitution must be taught. The federal government's role according to the Constitution is, "to promote the general welfare and secure the blessings of liberty to ourselves and our posterity." The federal government has no place in the classroom except to support education financially and not in what our children should be taught. Promoting education should be accomplished by distributing the money equally to each state.

Allotting the money to school boards to use at their discretion is the responsibility of the states. Here, we as parents, grandparents, and all concerned citizens must get involved. We must control the curriculum at the local level to ensure that our children are learning our history and how we've become the hope of freedom around the world. We cannot continue to lead without knowing who we are and, that includes from where we came. We must work alongside our children to ensure they are being taught how to think, not what to think, that they are taught to have a strong work ethic and are held accountable to earn their grades and subsequent graduation if deserved.

We must be assured that our children learn what it means to be an American citizen. The values, ideals, and principles that we were raised by have been undermined for this generation by the schools. Our children have been taught from an early age that they should call the police on their parents, pitting the children against their parents at their discretion, regardless of their immaturity. Our children are told that their parents can't hit them or they can call the police. A young child does not understand the difference between discipline and child abuse. This is an infringement of our parental rights as to how we choose to raise our children and, as such, is unconstitutional. It is intrusive and has been a weapon used by repressive regimes across the world to perpetuate their power.

We must ensure that our laws are in line with our values and morals and do not infringe on our rights to ensure our children learn respect and know the difference between right and wrong. As a child, I was taught to live right and stay out of trouble. I was more afraid to come home to my parents if I had gotten into trouble of any kind than the actual trouble I faced in school. We were taught to respect our elders, our teachers, and the police. We would never bring shame to our family by misbehaving at school badly enough for them to send a note home or needing to have the police call or bring us home to our parents. We were aware there would be consequences for our behavior, both inside and outside of our homes that we dreaded. Our schools should be teaching our children to respect their parents or guardians. Children need to learn respect, a commodity sorely lacking in our society today.

Our schools also need to challenge our kids to reach their potential in subjects such as math and science, so innovation can continue to be the edge America has to fuel our economy and lead the world to a better future. This is what has enabled us to enjoy a standard of living that is the envy of the world. The United States has always been a country of endless opportunities for all who seek to pursue their dreams, free to work hard. With perseverance, they can succeed according to their God-given talents and skills.

Lastly, the schools need to instill in our children the understanding that our Constitution is based on a single, undeniable fact, one that our Founding Fathers understood well: the rights of every individual come from God and, as such, cannot be taken away by anyone. The government is in place to protect our rights and cannot infringe on them. The government is in place to serve the wishes of the people and to follow the supreme law of the land, the Constitution. Thomas Jefferson put it so eloquently when he said, "God who gave us life gave us liberty. Can the liberties of a nation be secure when we have removed a conviction that these liberties are the gift of God?Indeed I tremble for my country when I reflect that God is just, that his justice cannot sleep forever. Commerce between master and slave is despotism. Nothing is more certainly written in the book of fate than that these people are to be free. Establish a law for educating the common people. This it is the business of the state and on a general plan."[1] This quote can be found at the Jefferson Memorial on panel number three. We, as citizens cognizant of our great legacy, must ensure it is passed on to our children, that the values that have always made America great come from our faith in divine providence and its role in our blessings that have led to our achievements as a nation under God.

Notes

1. Thomas Jefferson: Notes on Virginia Q.XVIII, 1782. ME 2:227 http://etext.virginia.edu/jefferson/quotations/jeff0100.htm, accessed July 31, 2010.

CHAPTER 15

Entitlement Programs

Entitlement programs have been sold to us as the duty of a compassionate people to take care of each other. The problem with that, however, is that we are giving money to the government, and they have mismanaged and left these programs in danger of insolvency. Another issue with these programs is they are misguided in that they do not address the problems, just the symptoms. Welfare programs, Medicaid, and Medicare not only are costing the taxpayers an exorbitant amount of money, fueling our national deficit annually, but they are also putting us in danger of bankrupting our nation. We have always been a compassionate people who have taken better care of each other than the government has proved to be able to in moments of great need.

Social Security is another entitlement program gone awry. It was in 1935 that Social Security, as we know it, was signed into law by Franklin D. Roosevelt under the title of Old Age, Survivors and Disability Insurance Program. The House vote had some bipartisan support, with 284 Democrats and 81 Republicans voting for the bill. He said, "It would act as a protection for future administrations against the necessity of going deeply into debt to furnish relief to the needy." He went on to say, "This is a law that will take care of human needs at the same time providing the United States an economic structure of vastly greater soundness."[1] It currently is the world's largest government-run program and the largest expenditure in the budget.[2] It is unconscionable to leave such a huge debt to our children and those beyond.

Then we must assess the program's finances, what we have paid and what has been paid for us by our employers, and start from there. We need to realize what we have heard for quite some time: we need to take control of how we manage our retirement. We cannot sell out our children's, grandchildren's, and posterity's future freedom and ability to do their best as a generation. America has always left each succeeding generation with more than the previous, but now we must look at the cost and what we can afford. We have no right to saddle our posterity with a program that is unsustainable. We must be honest with ourselves.

Another entitlement program was the enactment of Medicare. This idea was initially offered by President Harry Truman in 1945, but he was unsuccessful in his efforts to get it passed. Medicare was signed into law in 1965 by Lyndon B. Johnson. Again, there was limited bipartisan support with the House, vote of 248 Democrats and 65 Republicans.

The Medicare program is also on the brink of insolvency, with a current estimated $89 trillion in unfunded liabilities. When you add the unfunded liabilities of Social Security and Medicare together, there is an estimated $107 trillion of debt in 2009 and climbing.[3] That equates to $900,000 owed by each American household.

Entitlement programs may not always help those they are intended to help, because they can give individuals no reason to better themselves and ingrain dependence on others. Ben Franklin said it best when he wrote in November of 1776, "I think the best way of doing good to the poor, is not making them easy in poverty but leading or driving them out of it. In my youth, I travelled much, I observed in different countries that the more public provisions were made for the poor, the less they provided for themselves and of course became poorer. And on the contrary, the less was done for them, the more they did for themselves and became richer."[4] This speaks to a deep understanding of human nature. We are not going to work hard to better ourselves if there is no reward for our efforts. This is why history has taught us again and again that socialism and communism are bound to fail and why America's capitalist economic system has allowed us to lead the world into prosperity.

The recently passed Health Care Reform legislation is another example of a huge government entitlement program. The bill itself, and the way it was crafted and passed into law against the wishes of the American people, is unconstitutional and must be fought as an infringement on our individual liberties and states' rights. This is an attack on our freedoms and our way of life, as well as our system of representative government. This program, unlike its predecessors, was passed on strictly party lines, with 219 Democrats voting for the bill in the House and 210 against, including all Republicans.

The impassioned speech by House Minority Leader John Boehner from Ohio leading up to the vote was both eloquent and perfectly articulated. This was a flawed bill, devoid of transparency, filled with deals hammered out behind closed doors, with provisions added to buy the votes necessary for passage. Unfortunately, the Republican Party found its voice after it was too late to stop the bill. This bill equates to larger government and less individual liberty. Government must be reigned in, as the Constitution was intended, and our individual liberties must be protected by our elected officials, who have not kept their oath to preserve, protect, and defend the Constitution. In the upcoming elections, we must clear the House and Senate of those who have betrayed our trust and vote in candidates who will follow the Constitution and return this great country to its proper course, one in which any man, woman, or child is free to take hold of their own destiny, free of government intrusion as our Founding Fathers so wisely put in place.

Entitlement programs are a greater evil than solution to help those in need in our society. We must hold true to our American values of hope, faith, and charity. We must take care of each other like we always have. This nation has a proud history of rising to any challenge put in front of us, whether it be a natural disaster at home or abroad, the rise of tyranny, or any threat to the principles of freedom and the right of self-determination. Americans have always answered the call throughout the world. If we are to regain our rightful place in the world, we must continue our heritage free of the burden of these entitlement programs that threaten our very existence as a free and sovereign nation.

Notes

1. Franklin Roosevelt
http://www.ssa.gov/history/fdrstmts.html#signing, accessed July 31, 2010.

2. Social Security
http://en.wikipedia.org/wiki/Social_Security_(United_States), accessed March 7, 2010.

3. Social security and Medicare unfunded liabilities
http://www.ncpa.org/pub/ba662, accessed July 31, 2010.

4. Ben Franklin On the Price of Corn and Management of the Poor, 1776
http://www.founding.com/founders_library/pageID.2146/default.asp, accessed July 31, 2010.

CHAPTER 16

Spending Accountability

Here we must, as Americans, come together and realize that to reach our true potential as a people, we must share common values. You don't buy what you can't afford; you save until you've earned it. On this simple statement, I believe we should all agree. We owe it to our posterity to right our country's course and leave future generations with a better America than the one we found. We can never expect to do that if we continue down the path of fiscal irresponsibility. We must live within our means as a nation. We need to review the budget and reduce the funds needed to run our bloated and inefficient bureaucracies. This includes government entities that have grown intrusive and work to the detriment of the citizens of our nation.

We must also keep in mind that we must demand a balanced budget with domestic cuts, especially in times of war. We as a nation have become soft; we grumble as our brave men and women stand in harm's way ready to sacrifice their lives, while we sacrifice nothing at home. World War II was won with the sacrifice and bravery of our troops, but the people at home sacrificed as well. Certain items were rationed, and the citizens did not complain; they knew they were doing their part to assist the war effort. Thousands of brave men and women died to wrest a single island from enemy hands, just to move closer to victory. The cost in American lives was staggering, but we did not shy away from our duty. We can do no less, lest history judge us as unworthy to carry on the American tradition.

Spending accountability is not limited to the federal government but to all state, county, and local governments as well. We must decide what we truly need from the things we were told we could have but that have proven to be unsustainable. Is it not about time that we learn to hold our leaders accountable, as well as ourselves? Do we teach our children self-reliance and the value of hard work and education as the keys to their future? I believe Americans want their children to succeed and not expect to be taken care of by a huge, intrusive, federal government at the price of our God-given liberties.

Fiscal responsibility must come now, as there is no time to lose. Our debt puts our nation in a position of relying on others to sustain our current way of life. Working together, we must face the realities and find a better way. If we must sacrifice now for the sake of our posterity, it is our duty to do so. The American dream must be restored, along with our faith. Faith is what allowed this country to win its freedom against seemingly insurmountable odds against the most powerful military in the world at the time.

We have since grown so strong militarily that no foreign power can match our troops and their capabilities. We must continue to ensure our armed forces are equipped with the technological edge that has allowed us to be the guardians of peace and the free world. The only thing that can destroy us is our own greed and avarice. We cannot allow our nation to be destroyed from within by ill-advised, naive, or even nefarious leaders who are setting us on a course to the destruction of our republic. Demand that our politicians on every level be frugal in the ways they spend our money. We need to shrink our government and hold it accountable to the will of the people they are paid handsomely to represent.

We must regain our economic strength and bring jobs back to America. This can only be accomplished by keeping government out of the way of our true strength: the innovative, entrepreneurial spirit that has made this country great. The free market system is what has given us our strength. We must stop the practice of rewarding bad behavior. As children, we all learned this lesson. We should not give taxpayer money to corporations that are mismanaged. We should be rewarding success not failure. We learn from our mistakes, and that is what makes us better. No longer can we stand back and allow the federal government to overstep its boundaries and take over large corporations, controlling our choices.

We must also make use of the abundance God has so kindly bestowed on us. We must use our own resources, leading to energy independence and the job growth we so desperately need. Weaning ourselves from sending our hard-earned money to countries that are not allies or even friendly must begin now. Exploration and use of our abundant natural resources, coupled with investment for future technologies, will strategically give our nation a competitive edge until we can make oil dependence a thing of the past. We must ensure our elected leaders do everything in their power to stop the out-of-control spending and invest in keeping America's people working toward self-reliance in every measure. All spending measures must be reviewed and defined as being in our national interest, being cost-efficient, and in line with our national values. The days of a free lunch are over; we must instill in people the work ethic that built this great nation.

CHAPTER 17

The Federal Reserve System

The idea of a centralized bank has been around since before our founding. In fact, it was a point of controversy for our Founding Fathers. Thomas Jefferson was adamantly opposed to the idea. He said, "The incorporation of a bank and the powers assumed by legislation doing so have not, in my opinion, been delegated to the United States by the Constitution. They are not among the powers specially enumerated."[1]

Nevertheless, we have had one throughout most of our history.

Congress first tried to establish a centralized bank in 1781, but its charter was revoked by the Pennsylvania legislature. This effectively blocked it from truly being centralized and led to its demise. This occurred under the Articles of Confederation, before the U.S. Constitution was written and ratified.

The First Bank of the United States was chartered in 1791 for twenty years by the Congress. It was proposed by the secretary of the treasury, Alexander Hamilton, who insisted it must be a private institution. To fund it, an excise tax was enacted, which led to the Whiskey Rebellion. The bank lasted until 1811, when it was shut down under President James Madison. The vote to end its charter was sixty-five to sixty-four in the House of Representatives and was passed in the Senate when a tie was broken by Vice President George Clinton.

President James Madison later reinstated it in the form of the

Second Bank of the United States for another twenty-year charter. When Andrew Jackson, who was opposed to the bank, was elected president, he withdrew the federal government's funds from the bank. The bank responded by withholding funds, thereby contracting the money supply and leading to a recession, which the president of the bank, Nicholas Biddle, blamed on President Jackson and his economic policies. There would be no central bank in the United States from 1837 to 1862. This was followed by passage of the National Banking Act in 1863, which set up a system of national banks. This was also relatively short lived, as various bank runs made the idea of a central bank popular and led to the creation of the Federal Reserve System.

The Federal Reserve Act was signed into law by President Woodrow Wilson on December 23, 1923. It was intended to protect the economy, yet six years later, America endured the Great Depression. Prominent economists, including current Federal Reserve Chairman Ben Bernanke, believe the actions of the Federal Reserve directly led to the Great Depression.[2] The opinion is that in an effort to discourage speculative activity on Wall Street, the Fed contracted the money supply. Instead of protecting the American people, it led to our greatest social and financial crisis to date. Ironically, the same situation we faced then is what we are facing now, with Wall Street again being demonized. The stock market losses we faced recently hit all of the American people hard, as our retirement plans are at least partially in the stock market. Unfortunately, those hit the hardest were those who were close to retiring, as most of us watched a significant percentage of our 401K plans disappear.

The most recent stock market crash hurt us, but what followed was even worse, as the housing market crashed, robbing many Americans of the equity in their homes. The irony here is that the former Federal Reserve chairman Alan Greenspan had warned us for years of a housing bubble that would eventually burst. The policies enacted freeing credit for mortgages created an atmosphere of speculative buying, as people invested in real estate, expecting to continue to reap huge windfall profits on resale. Instead, there were people owing more on their mortgages than the properties were worth and what they could afford to pay.

The Federal Reserve is an independent entity with a huge amount of power and little accountability to the American people. There are efforts under way to audit the Federal Reserve in Congress, which should be done as a first step of bringing this institution back under our control. We must embrace these efforts and support the idea that the institution's actions be transparent to the American people. Its leaders must be held accountable, and then an informed decision on the future of the Federal Reserve System must be made. This is too important an area to be left in the hands of a few people to act on our behalf, leaving us with the consequences. It is clear additional oversight is required, and the future charter should be reviewed, revised more often, and then revised or revoked as necessary to ensure its actions are in our national interest.

Notes

1. Thomas Jefferson: Opinion on Bank, 1791. ME 3:146
http://etext.virginia.edu/jefferson/quotations/jeff1325.htm, accessed
July 31, 2010.

2. History of centralized banking in the United States
http://en.wikipedia.org/wiki/Federal_Reserve_System, accessed March
7, 2010.

CHAPTER 18

Summary

My purpose in writing this book was to encourage American citizens to consider, discuss, and hopefully reach consensus on a commonsense path to wresting back control of our government, back from the special interests that are plaguing our political process. I believe that we need to be educated and informed, as we face the decisions that will shape the future of our nation. We must understand who we are as a people from a historical perspective and how we are in a battle for the soul and future of our great republic. We must have an understanding of the Declaration of Independence, the U.S. Constitution, and the liberties we have enjoyed as a result of the restrictions the Constitution placed on our federal government to interfere in our ability to pursue life, liberty, and the pursuit of happiness.

We must, as I stated previously, engage in the political process and ensure our voices are heard and those who would take away our freedoms be confronted and defeated at the ballot box. We can remain silent no longer. We must raise our voices forevermore. To quote Martin Luther King Jr., "Our lives begin to end the day we remain silent about things that matter."[1] How many of us feel that government is unresponsive to our needs, unrepresentative of our views, denies us our basic liberties, and gives us no voice or ability to seek redress from unfair practices? As I speak to Americans across this great land, it seems to me many are angry that our government does not respect us as capable of making intelligent decisions. Instead, they tell us they know better than we do what's in our best interest.

Much to the detriment of people where this has occurred, the concept of kings has been replaced in our time with the reality of dictators and ruling classes deciding what is in the best interest of the masses. The history of the world is clear: no government of this type has succeeded or proved a boon to its populace. To the contrary, it has ruined many nations. The path of individual freedom and the fate of mankind rest on the success of our republic as set forth in our Constitution. Our elected officials need to understand that their powers come from the consent of the American people, and they must be beholden to our wishes. They must also understand that government is to be limited in its scope and accountable to us. They must honor our historical values and uphold their oaths to preserve, protect, and defend the Constitution. Nationally elected officials must put country before local considerations when they vote on legislation.

Our historical values have always espoused our duty to God and country. The Founding Fathers did not intend to remove God from government but, more precisely, the opposite. They actively sought His wisdom, guidance, and blessings to allow us to proclaim the rights that God gave every human being. They fought to procure them for themselves and their posterity. We live in precarious times. There is a gathering of potential threats to us, our way of life, and our liberties. We need to expect our elected officials to represent the majority of us who are God-fearing and moral, and who have faith that our fate is always in His hands. They must realize our freedoms come from the Creator, and their solemn duty is to protect them for us. They must understand what the Founding Fathers meant when George Washington said in the first official presidential proclamation on October 3, 1789, "It is the duty of all nations to acknowledge the providence of Almighty God, to obey his will, to be grateful for his benefits, and humbly to implore his protection and favor."[2]

We must hold our candidates in the 2010 elections to a standard higher than ever before. They must pledge to work to rein in the size of government, abiding by not only the written Constitution but the intent of the Founding Fathers, a government that protected individual and states' rights. Freedom of speech is paramount, as is the right to peacefully assemble to hold our government accountable to the American people. They are called public servants for a reason: their power comes from us. When we feel they have not adequately represented our values and wishes, we reserve the right to raise our voices in righteous indignation. George Washington said, "If the freedom of speech is taken away then dumb and silent we may be led, like sheep to the slaughter."[3] Our potential candidates must understand that America's history is extraordinary, and they should not be apologizing for our great nation. We've gone from a largely agriculture society to defeat the preeminent military power in the world at the time based on a faith that God had given each of us inalienable rights, and He would see us through to become the preeminent power in the world.

Our candidates must understand the country's deeply religious faith on which our government was founded and pledge to follow our Founding Fathers in seeking God's blessings and wisdom to keep our republic strong and free, while protecting the written text and intentions of our Founding Fathers. Here, I would urge you to read George Washington's Farewell Address, which so eloquently gives voice to the place of religion, God, and morality in our government.

The next condition to which we must hold our elected officials accountable is the imposition of mandatory term limits. This is imperative if we are to diminish the role of special interest's money and undue influence in public matters. Federally elected officials must put the interests of the nation as a whole above regional or local matters. This is not to diminish their accountability to their constituency but to uphold their oath to the Constitution. I believe that another avenue would be amendments to the states' constitutions, setting term limits on all levels of public service. I would also suggest local- and state-level candidates additionally pledge to give us the right of recall if a politician does not meet our expectations and breaks his or her word and bond with constituents. This should apply to everyone, from the governor on down, to the U.S. Representative or Senator from that state.

Term limits also allow more citizens the opportunity to engage in the political process. We need to become personally involved in all levels of government, especially local- and state-level positions. We must be vigilant of school boards, local, county, and state agencies. We must make sure they follow and promote our values and adequately educate our children for the challenges they will face as they prepare to take their place as the next generation of Americans. They must have the knowledge of who we are, so our country can continue to provide the world with the leadership it so desperately needs from us. It is our legacy and our cause to advance the cause of freedom and liberty to all who would seek it.

George Washington told us this in his Farewell Address as he stepped down from public service:

> Profoundly penetrated with this idea, I shall carry it with me to my grave, as a strong incitement to unceasing vows that Heaven may continue to you the choicest tokens of its beneficence; that your union and brotherly affection may be perpetual; that the free constitution, which is the work of your hands, may be sacredly maintained; that its administration in every department may be stamped with wisdom and virtue; then, in fine, the happiness of the people of these States, under the auspices of liberty, may be made complete, by so careful a preservation and so prudent a use of this blessing, as will acquire to them the glory of recommending it to the applause, the affection, and adoption of every nation, which is yet a stranger to it.[4]

We must look for candidates who seek not to enrich themselves but rather to pay patriotic service to their country. Congressional pay, benefits, and all matters of fund-raising must be reviewed in public. The incomes of our politicians should be transparent to reinforce the public trust that our elected officials are doing our business and not their own. Our candidates must hold true to their campaign promises and work in the full view of the American people. They must end any additional pay raises until the government is running on a surplus, has made us financially independent, and the pay of the average American citizen is much more proportionate to their pay. Benefits should be earned in line with what working American citizens would get over time of service.

The American citizens that I have spoken with all seem to agree that the Constitution must be more closely followed. The will and intentions of the Founding Fathers should be adhered to, and individual liberties and states' rights should be strengthened, while the federal government is held to its limited power. This includes a census that carries out only its constitutionally mandated task: to count the citizens of voting age at the time of the census to apportion the Congress by state, thus shifting the electoral map. The 2010 census did not ask if you were a citizen, the one question it was intended to ask so congressional seats could be properly apportioned based on changes in a state's population. Congressional redistricting should be based on a legal count as required by law. This census did not fulfill its duty and is inaccurate, thus rendering redistricting impossible.

The key to restoring our republic and its ideals of individual liberties granted by God is to rein in the great discontent sweeping across our land in a coherent and straightforward manner. We must give direction to our candidates who seek our support. To begin with, they must realize our nation's dependence on God's grace and blessings to allow us to keep and spread the cause of liberty.

The Constitution must be followed, and the Bill of Rights protected and preserved. Freedom from a federal religion, the freedom of speech in every form, and freedom of assembly are the beginning. Not freedom from religion but freedom from the ability of the federal government to enforce a national religion. The freedom to follow our own hearts, consciences, and souls to what we perceive as the Creator—free from government interference. Ben Franklin and George Washington both eloquently put their respect of God into words. Franklin, in response to being asked what he thought was the American religion, said, "Here is my creed I believe in one God, the creator of the universe. That he governs it by his Providence. That He ought to be worshipped. That the most acceptable service we render to Him is in doing good to His other children. That the soul of a man is immortal, and will be treated with justice in another life respecting its conduct in this."[5] George Washington said, "It is impossible to rightly govern a nation without God and the Bible."[6]

It is impossible for the government to do our work and regain our trust when they can govern out of the sight of the American people. Sunshine laws and legislation in plain language are essential to the kind of transparency we must demand of our elected officials. Lobbying should be strictly limited to advocacy, and there should be no money or help in election campaign matters allowed. Then and only then will our politics be free of the corruption that plagues our system.

Our government must meet its obligation to keep us free through unparalleled strength. National security and homeland security are paramount and will never be attained until our borders are secured once and for all. Illegal immigration must be stopped, while legal immigration can continue to add to the diversity of ideas that have made this country great. This is the promise of America, to take in those who seek refuge from tyranny, intolerance, and the lack of liberties we so proudly enjoy. Part of this is to regain our financial and energy independence from foreign interests and governments. We cannot be a debtor nation. As Franklin said, "The borrower is a slave to the lender and the debtor to the creditor."[7] We must control our own destiny free of the influence of others. We must insist on a path where American resources are used to fuel our way of life and jump-start our economy by providing jobs.

Balanced budgets, review of foreign aid, and the elimination of government entitlement programs grown out of control. This seems so much to ask, especially of our elderly, who have selflessly given so much to us. Yet, deep in our hearts, we know we will do all we can to take care of our elders, while trying to salvage our children's future. It is not within the scope of the government's responsibility, and limited by the Constitution, to expect to be taken care of from cradle to grave. That is the task of liberty: to allow each of us to choose our own path and shape our own destiny. That is God's gift to humanity: the right to choose our own course by granting each of us the individual right to life, liberty, and the pursuit of happiness. This course of fiscal responsibility is essential to ensuring our nation not only survives, but that it thrives as well.

Finally, the Federal Reserve System must be reviewed and held accountable, reformed with public transparency, and possibly dissolved. This should begin with a full audit of the Federal Reserve and the making accountable of those who are charged with its decision-making processes and the consequences of those actions or inactions in times of need. Then we can decide if it is in our national interest.

I will end here with a challenge to the disaffected, the angry, those moved to peaceful protest for the first time. The Tea Party has been ignored, marginalized, and slandered by those who do not understand it. Their detractors believe it is all about taxes, but it is much more than that. The Tea Party consists of people who seek to restore the Constitution and slash the size, scope, and influence of an intrusive government. I believe that we have laid out and hopefully given voice and direction to the American people rising up at this moment in history and choosing the road of self-sacrifice to a cause greater than ourselves. To fight for the right to keep our country true to its historical values, while holding true to its roots. To return our government to its rightful place as a champion of protecting and promoting individual liberty. To understand and fulfill its role as an instrument to keep the states together for the common good, without infringing on their sovereignty or our rights.

America, once again history is calling on us, testing us, as will happen by necessity as each generation must face its moment of truth and either continue the American way or lose the world's best chance for justice, liberty, and freedom for all. This is our moment; this is our time. We stand at the crossroads of history. We will be judged by our children and the world by how we respond. We must unite and rise above the slander, greed, and avarice that threaten us. We must choose wisely in these elections, or it may be too late. Stand up, be heard, and make a difference. Stop the erosion of our Constitution and the rise of a government not representative of our intended system of government based on the principles of truth, liberty, and the pursuit of happiness for all of its citizens. Go out and make a difference. It is our duty.

Notes

1. Martin Luther King%2C Jr.. BrainyQuote.com, Xplore Inc, 2010. http://www.brainyquote.com/quotes/quotes/m/martinluth103526.html, accessed August 1, 2010.

2. George Washington's 1789 Thanksgiving Proclamation http://www.inlightimes.com/archives/2008/11/gems.htm, accessed March 25, 2010

3. George Washington. BrainyQuote.com, Xplore Inc, 2010. http://www.brainyquote.com/quotes/quotes/g/georgewash146824.html, accessed August 1, 2010.

4. George Washington's farewell address http://gwpapers.virginia.edu/documents/farewell/transcript.html

5. Letter to Ezra Smith, March 9, 1790 http://www.worldpolicy.org/globalrights/religion/franklin-religion.html, accessed August 1, 2010

6. George Washington. BrainyQuote.com, Xplore Inc, 2010. http://www.brainyquote.com/quotes/quotes/g/georgewash383981.html, accessed August 1, 2010.

7. Ben Franklin, *The Way to Wealth* http://itech.fgcu.edu/faculty/wohlpart/alra/franklin.htm#Way, accessed July 31, 2010.